Byways, Boots and Blisters – A History of Walkers and Walking

Byways, Boots and Blisters – A History of Walkers and Walking

Bill Laws

SUTTON PUBLISHING

First published in the United Kingdom in 2008 by
The History Press · Cirencester Road · Chalford · Stroud ·
Gloucestershire · GL6 8PE

British Library Cataloguing in Publication Data
A catalogue record for this book is available from the British Library.

ISBN 978 0 7509 4592 9

Typeset in Photina MT
Typesetting and origination by
The History Press Limited.
Printed and bound in England.

CONTENTS

ACKNOWLEDGEMENTS   8

'THE GREAT AFFAIR IS TO MOVE'   10

CHAPTER 1 – FIRST FOOTERS   13

Thomas Coryate   13

Mr Bos, drover   20

Ben Jonson   25

William Lithgow   28

Foster Powell   33

Footnote: Walking Boots   37

Captain Robert Barclay   38

Alfred Watkins   46

CHAPTER 2 – DEVOTED WALKERS   53

John Bunyan   53

Footnote: What Walkers Wear   58

Pastor Moritz   60

Rev'ds Bingley, Williams and Warner   67

Francis Kilvert   74

Canon Cooper   81

CHAPTER 3 – POETS IN MOTION   89
'Three persons and one soul'   89
Samuel Coleridge   92
William Wordsworth   99
Dorothy Wordsworth   106
William Hazlitt   112
Thomas De Quincey   119
Edward Thomas   125
Footnote: The Rucksack   133

CHAPTER 4 – BRINGING IT TO BOOK   136
John Taylor   136
William Hutton   142
Ellen Weeton   149
Footnote: Bloomers   156
George Borrow   158
Robert Louis Stevenson   168
Hilaire Belloc   174
William Hudson   180

CHAPTER 5 – A WALK ON THE WILD SIDE   187
Leslie Stephen   187
Benny Rothman   196
Footnote: The Devil's Rope   205
Tom Stephenson   206
Stephen Graham   217
Herbert Gatliff   226

CHAPTER 6 – ROUTE-MASTERS AND RECORD BREAKERS   236
Hugh Munro and William Poucher   236
'A.Walker'   241

Frank Noble   249
Footnote: The Stile   256
Trailblazers   258
Record breakers   264

Further Reading   268
Index   274

ACKNOWLEDGEMENTS

Walking is both a solitary and a companionable exercise. I have no-one to thank but the hills and wild weather for the former. However I owe a debt of gratitude to my walking mates: Jerry, Jon, Michelle, Mike, Leslie, and Stef for the germ of an idea; to Roger Calow for our sojourns in Wales and the Outer Hebrides; to Nic Millington and Archie for our Offa's Dyke journey; and my fellow footpath wardens, Hugh Bryant and Wendy Harvey. My thanks to my family, Abby, Sarah, Kahlia and Rosie, are tempered by an apology for all those short cuts that did not work out.

I am grateful too to Bobbie Blackwell of Herefordshire Lore, Rebe Beck and Wendy Smith from the Offa's Dyke Centre, John Burland, the Estate of A. Wainwright and Pauline Brocklehurst from Animal Rescue, Cumbria at the Wainwright Shelter, Karl and Keith Bushby, Len Clark, Terry Court, Derby City Council, the Edward Thomas Fellowship, Robin Field, Dan French and staff at the Ramblers' Association, Filey Museum, Elizabeth Gatliff, Elaine

Goddard, Roger Hinchcliffe, Eve Huskins, Joe Hillaby, Andy Johnson of Logaston Press, members of the Kilvert Society, Elspeth Loades, Lizzie Lane of BBC Hereford and Worcester, Eve Lichfield, Jaqueline Mitchell, June Noble, Jean O'Donnell, David Petts, John Poucher, Barry Ray, Ann Soutter and the George Borrow Society, Peter Elkington from Rydal House and Gardens, Ali Kuosku and Silva Sweden AB, Glen Storhaug, Gavan Tredoux (www.galton.org), Wigan Heritage Services, the Youth Hostels Association (England and Wales) and especially their patient archivist Trevor Key, staff at the British Library, Bristol City Library and Herefordshire Libraries especially Robin Hill, volunteers at the Gatliff Hebridean Hostels Trust especially John Humphries and Frank Martin, the The Company of Watermen and Lightermen of the River Thames, and my agent, Chelsey Fox of Fox and Howard.

'THE GREAT AFFAIR
IS TO MOVE'

Between our first faltering steps as a toddler and the time when age or infirmity finally axe our legs from under us, walking is our liberation. 'The great affair', declared Robert Louis Stevenson, 'is to move.'

Some people walk because it's good for them. It gets those endomorphins going. Ignoring Hilaire Belloc's insistence (*An Anthology for Walkers*) that 'the detestable habit of walking for exercise warps the soul' they step out on the gym treadmill, the approving words of George Macaulay Trevelyan ringing in their ears. 'I have two doctors,' he wrote in *Clio, A Muse and other Essays Literary and Pedestrian* (1913). 'My left leg and my right.'

Some, like the estimated 18 million Britons who regularly enjoy a summer's day stroll, walk for the pure pleasure of it, often in company, occasionally in solitude. George Borrow and the sociable socialist Benny Rothman (one of his strolls on Kinder Scout cost him three months in prison) were gregarious and walked to meet people. The great Alfred Wainwright walked to escape them.

Some of our pedestrian heroes walked further than

most. In the nineteenth century Captain Barclay was reputed to have walked over 130 miles in twenty-four hours, while William Wordsworth was said (by Thomas De Quincey who walked his own fair share of English miles) to have walked almost 18,000 miles by the age of sixty-five. And while Birmingham's William Hutton, who trotted up to Hadrian's Wall and back, a distance of 600 miles, in his seventy-eighth year, celebrated his ninetieth birthday with a ten mile stroll, Thomas Coryate and William Lithgow walked themselves to death.

There are those who walked shorter distances, yet still enjoyed themselves. The farther you go the less you know, maintained Lao Tsu in *Tao Te Ching*. The Rev'd Francis Kilvert, one of a congregation of clerics who scaled the Welsh hills, was never happier than when he was 'villaging about' visiting his flock and watching out for pretty parishioners. William Hudson, meanwhile, was content to be, as he called himself, a traveller in little things.

Many had a particular reason for taking a hike. Foster Powell walked for money, Samuel Coleridge for literary inspiration, Ben Jonson, despite his size, for literary posterity and Richard Long for his art. London's Stephen Graham walked to see where the compass would take him, while Frank Noble and Tom Stephenson walked to blaze new trails, Offa's Dyke and the Pennine Way respectively.

It follows that, like the Inuit with his arsenal of words for snow and the Celt with more than a few names for rain, the English speaker should have inherited a rich lexicon of walking words. We stroll and wander. We saunter and meander. We amble and ramble. We hike and we tramp. Footsore finally, we trudge and plod home to bed. (Or to our computers – sharing the slog on a blog is a growing phenomenon and walkers' websites ring with anxieties: 'What type of food do I need on the Coast to Coast?' 'How can I prepare for 60 miles of the Pembrokeshire Coast Path on my 60th birthday?')

Young walkers fret about fitness levels; older walkers worry about staying the course. But with so many pedestrians covering so many miles there is no shortage of sensible advice from what to carry (whiskey for wet feet, advised Canon Cooper; an umbrella to avoid being mistaken for a robber, suggested George Borrow; a collar and tie in case you need to visit the bank, advised Graham) to training for the journey (walk twenty miles a day with plenty of purging sweats, counseled the nineteenth-century Walter Thom; carry an overweight rucksack around with you, recommended John Hillaby. On the journey itself the relief of carrying a lighter pack would put a spring in your step).

Finally the act of walking can be a therapy in itself. While William Wordsworth found his poetic muse from wandering, many others have found solace and a solution by following the old Latin proverb *solvitur ambulando*. Sort it out through walking.

CHAPTER 1

FIRST FOOTERS

THOMAS CORYATE
'He went most on foot'

In the late summer of 1617 a small crowd gathered at the market cross in Odcombe, Somerset. They had come to hear the departing speech of local hero Thomas Coryate. The son of the village's late rector, Coryate was a dapper-looking Elizabethan with a generous head of swept-back hair, a trim beard and, if his portrait by William Hole is anything to go by, the look of a man curious about life. He satisfied that curiosity by walking. 'Of all the pleasures in the world travel is (in my opinion) the sweetest and most delightfull,' he once declared. He was small and lean, no doubt a consequence of constantly travelling 'mounted on a horse with ten toes' as his contemporary Bishop Fuller described him.

Eccentric Englishmen seem to have taken to walking long distances for pleasure long before other nationals. Thomas Coryate who wished to 'animate the learned to travel into outlandish regions' was one of the first on record. Revealing his travel plans to his fellow villagers that morning in 1617 Coryate declared himself bound for India by way of Greece, Palestine and Persia. On foot. He then presented his old walking shoes to the village church (hung in the porch they would attract curious visitors for decades after his death) and set out on the Yeovil road to Portsmouth with a last look back at friendly Odcombe. He would never return.

Nine years before on 14 May 1608, the then thirty-two year old had departed from Dover on his first major journey. 'There hath itched a very burning desire in me to survey and contemplate some of the chiefest parts of this goodly fabric of the world,' he explained. His father had died the year before, the proceeds of the will, possibly helping to fund his journey. He started his 1,975 mile circumnavigation of forty-five European cities first on the Dover ferry and then on horseback, but he completed the return journey on foot.

Coryate spent five months travelling and, at its conclusion, rushed home to record his recollections. The book took three years to write and proved, at first, impossible to publish. The interminable and long-winded title may have been partly to blame:

Coryate's Crudities Hastily gobbled up in Five Moneths travels in France, Savoy, Italy, Rhetia commonly called Grisons country, Helvetia alias Switzerland, some parts of High Journey and the Netherlands; Newly digested in the hungry aire of Odcombe in the County of Somerset and now dispersed to the nourishment of the travelling members of this Kingdome.

The contents, however, were revealing for Coryates, or the Odcombian legge-stretcher as he called himself, not only provided precise details of distances, places and peoples, but also such a store of entertaining anecdote that the book, when it did go to print, became a seventeenth-century sensation.

Coryate's Crudities provided the reader with more than a mere *hors d'ouevres* of the walker's world. He described being half drowned in a stream of horse urine (having inadvertently bedded down in the animal's straw) and enduring terrible sea sickness on the Channel crossing, (the graphic on the cover of *Crudities* depicted an Elizabethan lady throwing up on his head). He fled a group of Venetians who were intent, he was convinced, on forcibly circumcising him. Later he must resist the charms of a famous Venetian courtesan, Margarita Emiliana: 'As for thine eyes, shut them and turn them aside from these venerous Venetian objects,' he tells himself.

But this clergyman's son also proved to be a sensible journeymen, a traveller with an observant eye and an open mind. When he notes the Italians using

Thomas Coryate as depicted on the cover of his book by William Hole.

a 'little forke' with which to eat their meat (rather than risk contamination from unclean hands) he adopts the fork himself and is credited by some for introducing it into England. Walking and talking he hears Latin spoken in the more relaxed European mode and modifies his own pronunciation accordingly.

On his return he faced up to the writer's perennial problem: finding a publisher. Thomas Coryate was well educated and well connected. In his twenties having left Gloucester Hall, Oxford without a degree but with a good command of the classics, he played the happy fool at court with Prince Henry for he was 'always Tongue-Master of the company' according to Ben Jonson, while Bishop Fuller declared that 'sweatmeats and Coryate made up the last course on all court entertainments'. It was to friends like these, and influential acquaintances such as John Donne, Thomas Campion, the poet Drayton and the architect Inigo Jones, that Coryates now turned for help with his book. He extracted testimonials, mostly written in mocking verse and in a range of languages including Irish and Welsh, from more than sixty of them. These were published later as a book of 'panegyrick verses' in their own right, the *Odcombian Banquet.*

The reading public, small and select as it was, tucked into *Coryate's Crudities* with relish, so much so that Coryate rushed out a second book, *Coryate's Crambe, or his Colewort twice sodden* which added to his celebrity status as a walker.

But fame, even in the seventeenth century, brought with it its brickbats. John Taylor, who wrote the first account of a walking tour in Britain regularly mocked the 'Odcombian Deambulator, Perambulator, Ambler, Trotter' and the verbal feud continued between the two walkers with Taylor still hurling insults after Coryate had made his final journey, and ended up, as one friend put it, lodging in the final 'Field of Bones'.

When he left Odcombe in 1617, Coryate made his way through Greece, Palestine and Persia. By the autumn he had reached Mandu in central India and joined the first official English embassy 'a bedraggled little band . . . dancing attendance on the Murghal Emperor Jahangir', according to Charles Nicholl writing in the London Review of Books. The group included the ambassador, Sir Thomas Rose (an acquaintance from Coryate's days at Prince Henry's court) and the embassy chaplain, Edward Terry, whose quarters Coryate shared for a while. Travelling on foot and living frugally, Coryate expected to manage on a penny a day, but he was, by now, running short of funds. Employing his natural talents as a linguist, he composed a letter in word-perfect Persian, begging for alms and sent it to the Murghal emperor. Rose, the English Ambassador, was furious at this humiliating breach of etiquette from an embassy guest. The emperor, however, was amused and sent Coryate 100 rupees. It was sufficient to finance what would be Coryate's final walk that November.

The embassy chaplain, Edward Terry, had described in his *A Voyage to East India* (1655) how Coryate had fallen into a swoon after having walked the 2,700 miles from Jerusalem to Ajmer covering inhospitable terrain at the rate of 70 miles a week. Now, wrote Terry, he walked out of the embassy 'like a ship that hath too much sail and too little ballast'. Nevertheless Coryate, exhausted and suffering from dysentery, managed to reach Surat on the Gujurati coast. Meeting a group of fellow countrymen, Coryate called for aid and alcohol. They plied him with sack, a sherry-like dry wine. The wise walker knows that drinking alcohol after a long tramp, which has depleted their sugar levels, can result in dizziness or fainting. In Coryate's case it killed him.

'It increased his flux which he then had upon him. And this caused him within a few days, after his very tedious and troublesome travels (for he went most on foot) at this place to come to his journey's end,' wrote Rev'd Terry. 'Sic exit Coryatus, and so must all after him (to) . . . the Field of Bones, wherein our Traveller hath now taken up his lodging.'

MR BOS, DROVER
'There is not a public house between here and Worcester at which I am not known'

Coryate was unusual in that, as one of the 'panegyrick verses' celebrating his achievements put it,

> either without scrippe or bagge
> He used his ten toes for a nagge.

Gentlemen of Coryate's class were expected to travel on horseback or by carriage, not least for their own safety.

His pedestrianism marked him out as an eccentric. Not that there was anything wrong with eccentricity according to the Victorian traveller Mabel Sharman Crawford. Eccentricity was 'in truth, the mainspring of our national progress' and an 'element of character eminently productive, on the whole, of good,' she wrote in one of her travel books, *Through Algeria*.

However for most people in Coryate's and Crawford's time walking was a necessity and not a pleasure. Working men and women walked miles because there was no alternative. Some of the hardiest walkers were to be found among the drovers of western and northern Britain, tough individuals paid to deliver meat on the hoof to the city folk who ate it. This trade in livestock, which had been recorded in Britain by the Romans, saw men drive cattle, sheep, pigs, turkeys and geese from the highlands, where the animals had been raised, to the lowlands where they were rested,

The walking drover would average two miles an hour.

fattened and butchered. The drovers' tracks followed the lonely lines of the hills, skirting expensive toll roads and resting at the motorway service station of the day, the drovers' inn. A stand of trees at a remote farmhouse would signpost some overnight grazing while half-remembered names in the English countryside, Welsh lane or Scotch walk, celebrated the passage of the drovers and their beasts as they walked their way to market at an average speed of two miles an hour, their collies and corgis yapping at their heels.

Having delivered their animals, the drovers returned home carrying hard cash and gossip from abroad, and bolstering their reputation for being rough, tough and rugged individuals. In reality many made respectable names for themselves. Richard Moore-Colyer in his *Roads and Trackways of Wales* mentions men such as Edward Morus of Perthi Llwydion, who regularly walked his cattle the 300 miles or so from North Wales to the county of Essex, and who was also a respected seventeenth-century poet. Another, Dafydd Jones of Caeo, was a noted Nonconformist hymn writer in the eighteenth century. They were not all men of the pen and the chapel: in 1850 one Welsh drover strapped a man who owed him money, to the neck of an unbroken colt at Barnet Fair in Hertfordshire. The debt was apparently repaid when the colt had travelled less than five miles.

The modern drover, the person responsible for moving livestock from pen to pen within the market, still walks for a living, but the long distance drovers have died out. Although, as Moore-Colyer points out, 'many of the Lewises, Evanses and Williamses currently enjoying a good living as graziers in the Shires owe their prosperity to drover ancestors', the obituary writers of the provincial press rarely remembered the humble drover.

However one not especially endearing drover gave a brief account of himself when he shared a drink with an observant writer, himself a walker, in 1854 in North Wales. Mr Bos, a pig drover in his forties, bumped into Mr George Borrow at an Anglesey inn. He had a broad red face, grey eyes, a wide mouth and a strong set of teeth – Borrow, writing in *Wild Wales* might almost have been describing a prize horse. He was dressed in a pepper-and-salt coat 'of the Newmarket cut', corduroy breeches and brown top boots. He wore the broad, black, low-crowned hat typical of the drover and carried a heavy whale-bone whip with a brass head.

The discourse between Borrow and Bos, a simple man who might have comfortably featured in a Victorian comic novel, sheds a little light on the life of the drover. Bos claimed to have been through every

Walking was a
way of life for men
like Mac Higgins,
one of the last
of the Welsh
borders drovers.
(Brightwells)

town in England, maintained that 'there is not a
public house between here and Worcester at which
I am not known', and declared a marked preference
for Northampton, not because of the men who were
'all shoemakers, and of course quarrelsome and con-
tradictory', but for the women who were even more
'free and easy' than those of Wrexham. Bos assumed
that Borrow was a pig jobber or pig drover and was
curious to know how much a stone Borrow received
for his live pork when he visited Llanfair. Borrow
refutes the suggestion.

'Who but a pig-jobber could have business at Llanfair?' wonders the drover. In fact, he wonders, why should anyone having any business in the whole of Anglesey, save that the business be pigs or cattle? Borrow fires Bos up, telling him that one Ellis Wynn 'gives the drovers a very bad character, and puts them in Hell for their malpractices'. Mr Bos is again confused. He had last met Wynn, a man who could neither read nor write, at Corwen. He now determines to 'crack his head for saying so' the next time they meet. The mix-up between Wynn the Corwen pig jobber and Borrow's Wynn (a respectable clergyman) is left unresolved and the author abandons the conversation to eat his supper.

Many professional drovers like Mr Bos were reaching the end of their useful working lives in the 1850s, the railways depriving them of their trade. Another drover tells Borrow that he has stopped droving: 'Oh yes, given him up a long time, ever since domm'd railroad came into fashion.'

Yet some working men still walked their sheep along the drovers' trails up until, and shortly after, the Second World War. One, well known in the markets of South Wales and the borders, was a sheep dealer called Mac Higgins. The story goes that on one of his last journeys he spent a week driving a hundred and fifty ewes from Carmarthen to the Wednesday sheep market at Hereford. He reached the market in time for the sale, but the sheep failed to sell. Eventually Mac's father arrived and, hearing the news, went into one of the many market pubs to try and effect a sale. Finally, at half past eight at night, Mac's father emerged from the pub with good news and bad: he had clinched a deal. But the buyer was from Swansea four days droving back down the road to Carmarthen.

BEN JONSON
'A foot pilgrimage to Scotland'

In 1599 a former friend of William Shakespeare, Will Kemp, Morris-danced the 127 miles from London's Royal Exchange to Chaplefield in Norwich. With rest days and delays (snow blocked his way at Bury St Edmunds) the journey, celebrated in Kemp's *Nine Daies Wonder*, took a month. (In 2000 a Morris team danced a day off Kemp's record). Kemp's eccentric venture was the probable inspiration for Thomas Coryate's own pedestrian journeys, which, in turn, inspired England's greatest dramatist of the time, Ben Jonson: two years after Coryate's death Jonson took the unlikely step, several in fact, of walking from London to Scotland.

Jonson had known and admired Coryate. He had edited the 'panegyrick verses' for Coryate's *Odcombian Banquet* and hailed the writer as 'a great and bold carpenter of words'. Jonson, who for a century after his death was judged the better playwright when compared to Shakespeare, planned to write a book about his walk. He even had a working title, *A Discovery*. But in 1632 fire destroyed his library and the unpublished manuscript went up in smoke. What the manuscript might have revealed was how Jonson managed his 'foot pilgrimage' when, by his own admission, he was 'twenty stones less two pounds' (125 kg).

In June 1619 the forty-five year old Jonson stepped out of his London home and, supported by a stout walking stick, headed for Hatfield and Bedford, but with Edinburgh, 400 miles away, as his destination. Apart from the domestic detail that he bought a new pair of shoes in Darlington, little else is known of his journey.

When he reached Edinburgh he was given a civic reception. He stayed in the city for over a year collecting material for the intended book and lodging with a number of acquaintances including a poet, William Drummond of Hawthorn. It was Drummond who reported later that, notwithstanding Jonson's own advice in Volpone that 'calumnies are best answered with silence', the dramatist was suspicious of the motives of a fellow walker. This was John Taylor who had also walked from London to Edinburgh. While Jonson had followed the eastern route through Newcastle, Taylor had trudged along the western route by Carlisle. And his reputation had preceded him. Taylor's motives for starting the war of words with poor Coryate 'the Odcombian Deambulator' were to fuel publicity for his own efforts. Now, thought Jonson, Taylor intended to discredit his own pedestrian efforts. According to Drummond, Jonson was convinced that Taylor was 'sent along to scorn him'.

Ben Jonson walked from London to Edinburgh despite weighing 'twenty stones less two pounds'. (Mary Evans Picture Library)

When Taylor reached the Scottish capital Jonson arranged to meet his walking adversary. In the end Jonson seems to have enjoyed Taylor's company, even presenting the walker with two guineas to drink to the dramatist's health when the poet returned to London. Jonson himself eventually returned to London to work on the ill-fated *A Discovery*. This time, however, he carried himself and his 'monstrous belly' home on the coach.

WILLIAM LITHGOW
'I bequeathed . . . my feet to the hard bruising way'

Coryate's and Jonson's walks were quiet affairs in comparison to those of William Lithgow, a Scotsman who claimed to have walked 36,000 miles in nineteen years. 'During his travels he never mounted a horse, or put his foot into a carriage, or any description of vehicle whatever,' wrote one commentator. However, what Lithgow described as his 'pedestriall pilgrimages' brought him pleasure and pain, and highlighted the dangers facing the footsore, solo walker in the seventeenth century.

Born in Lanark around 1583, Lithgow started his wanderings from necessity rather than choice. Embroiled in an unwise love affair, he was attacked by members of his lover's family who cut off his ears. Lithgow fled the country before they amputated anything else. Having started traveling, he found it impossible to stop.

In 1614 Lithgow walked through the 'Orcadian and Zetlaudian Isles' (Orkney and Shetland) and then on through the Low Countries, Germany and France. He gave a full, although possibly exaggerated, account of the pedestriall pilgrimages in *The Totall Discourse of the Rare Adventures and Painefull Peregrinations of Long Nineteen Years Travayles*, published in 1632. During these peregrinations he was 'by seas suffering thrice shipwracke, by Land, in Woods and on Mountaynes often invaded; by ravenous Beasts, crawling and venemous Wormes daily incombred; by home-bred

Robbers and remote Savages; five times stripd to the skin.' All this before his disastrous encounter with the Spanish authorities, when he was crippled after being tortured both by the civil administrators for being a spy and by the Inquisition for being a heretic.

In *Rare and Painful Peregrinations* he described the pleasures of coffee drinking, the first person in England to do so; he tells of a pigeon post operating out of Aleppo to Baghdad and of a native obsession with the dried grape, or currant, in that land. He observed how the women of Cairo 'piss standing although the men cower low on their knees doing the same'. In Crete he tells of a certain herb which gilds the teeth of those who eat it. When he heard the story that a dog, thrown into the Grotto di Cane in Italy, would die in the sulphurous water, and yet recover when thrown into a nearby lake, he tried to persuade a passing dog

Lithgow was regularly beaten by 'home-made robbers'

owner to test the theory. Sensibly the owner refused. Lithgow then immersed himself in the Grotto waters and emerged unscathed. Impressed, the dog owner threw in his pet. It drowned and, despite frantic efforts, was not revived by the waters of the lake.

Whether he was being attacked by robbers, sought by slave traders or defrauded by inn keepers, Lithgow was the constant victim. When he landed in Constantinople, the Turkish captain of his ship bade him goodbye with a cry of 'Adios Christiano'. It prompted 'four French renegades to fell desperately upon me, blaspheming the name of Jesus and throwing me on the ground, beat me most cruelly.'

Occasionally he was saved from assault by his tobacco pouch, since 'the Turks take as kindly as though it had been a pound of gold, for they are excessively addicted to smoke as Dutchman are to the pot.' But the nicotine rush is not enough to save him when, walking in Moldavia, he is 'beset with six murderers.' Having robbed him of everything they leave him tied naked to a tree. 'I was left here in a trembling fear for wolves and wild boar till the morrow; where at last I was relieved by a company of herdsmen.'

In Venice he was forced to suspend his perambulations when he was pursued by a gang of felons. After hiding for several nights in the roof of the Earl of Tyrone's residence, he managed to scale the city walls and escape. He walked on through Italy, across the Alps and through the former Yugoslavia to reach the Mediterranean Isles and Greece. As a compensation for all his hardships he was presented with a timely gift of fifty 'gold zechins', enough to allow him to continue his 'sumptuous peregrinations.'

Lithgow walked on, crossing Greece and travelling down through the Middle East into Jerusalem where he joins company with three Dutch men. Apparently they had been drinking too much 'strong Cyprus wine without mixture of water' and, one by one, they fall terminally ill. Each on his death bed generously bequeathed him their personal fortunes making our hero richer by some 942 gold zechins and rings and 'tablets'. Lithgow finally returned to England after walking through Cairo, Alexandria, Malta, Italy and France. He brought home with him 'certain rare gifts and notable relicks' from Jordan and Jerusalem which, diplomatically, he presented to King James, the Queen and Prince Charles.

Lithgow was to profit from dead men's money a second time during his next ramble, this time through Europe to North Africa and back via Eastern Europe. At one point he stumbled upon two noblemen lying dead in a field, the victims of a duel. He helps himself to their money. 'It was mine that was last theirs; and to save the thing that was not lost, I travelled that day thirty miles further to Terra Nova,' he recorded cheerfully.

It was thanks to experiences like these William Lithgow became a celebrity walker, regularly invited, in exchange for a traveller's tale or two, to dine with nobility. He was a welcome face at the English court and, as a consequence, Lithgow travelled under royal patronage on his next walk. Carrying letters of recommendation from King James he headed off on a hike to Ethiopia by way of Ireland and Spain. But the King's protection failed him when, in Spain, he was arrested as a spy and tortured, first by the civil authorities and then by the Inquisition. He was released only when news of his incarceration reached the English consul. The Scotsman, his injuries so severe that he could no longer walk, was sent back to England and, in 1621, in a bizarre spectacle, exhibited to the King and his court, laid out on a feather bed. Lithgow was dispatched to Bath spa for a cure, the King paying for his treatment, but the pedestrian's tribulations were not over yet.

King James arranged a meeting of reconciliation between Lithgow and the Spanish ambassador. However, when the two came face to face Lithgow could not contain his anger and he assaulted the ambassador. Dragged off by the palace guards, Lithgow was thrown into prison at Marshalsea for the attack.

After several fruitless attempts to secure compensation from the Spanish ambassador, Lithgow went wandering again. He failed in his attempt to walk to Russia, the severe weather defeating him. Little is known of his later years and he is thought to have died at the age of sixty-three after returning to live in his native Lanark in 1645. But, as one commentator recorded, his reputation lived on:

'He made it a rule, and strictly adhered to it, never to avail himself of any conveyance during a journey when he could accomplish it on foot, and his only deviation was in the case of crossing seas, rivers, or lakes.'

FOSTER POWELL,
'He never thirsted for money'

Foster Powell was a lean, mild-mannered Yorkshireman who 'departed this life' on April 15, 1793, aged fifty-nine according to *A Short Sketch of the Life of Mr Foster Powell*. Gathered at his graveside, the mourners at his funeral agreed that they were bidding goodbye to England's greatest pedestrian. Many also agreed that it was Foster's ill-fated attempt on his own speed record for walking from London to York and back the previous year, which finally killed him.

Powell, who was born in Horsforth, Yorkshire in 1734, performed his first speed walk, well dressed in a great coat and leather breeches, on a fifty mile 'ped' along the road out of Bath. He was, according to *A Short Sketch*, a lowly lawyer's clerk, a good man who 'never thirsted for money and felt a secret pleasure in being able at all times to fulfil his engagements.' Increasingly those engagements involved walking set distances as fast as he possibly could. While men such as Coryate, Lithgow and Jonson had popularised the long distance walk, Powell was helping to turn walking into one of the sport of kings, quite as popular in its time as its equine equivalent, horse racing.

Powell turned semi-professional, for example walking the 112 miles from Canterbury to London in under twenty-four hours. Journeys like these were walked as a wager, although the exercise seems to have brought him no great profit. His most famous walk, from London to York and back, earned him only £10 according to one authority (£40 according to another). It did, however, establish the ground rules for the new sport of 'heel and toe' or speed walking. 'Heel and toe' walking stipulated that the heel of the one foot should strike the ground before the toe of the other left it. And, as the fashion caught on, gentlemen raced to set walking records from town to town or over set distances of five, ten or fifty miles. The sporting public, ready to risk a shilling on the outcome, raced to meet them.

Powell made his name in 1773 at the age thirty-nine when he walked from London to York. There's nothing dramatic in that except that, on reaching York, he turned round and walked back to London, a total distance of 420 miles. Again the distance was not exceptional, but his speed was: he managed the journey in just over five and a half days, an average of seventy-two miles a day.

Powell left London for York on Monday 29 November, 1773, just after midday. He reached the city at two o'clock on the Wednesday fuelled on a diet of beer, tea and toast. According to *A Short Sketch*, 'he was very particular in his diet, seldom or ever ate any meat on his journeys, but mostly light food.' He allowed himself only five hours sleep and 'those from eleven o'clock at night'. Whether it was the food, the bed or both, Foster was constantly frustrated with his accommodation since 'he frequently met with great disappointment with his travels to those houses on the road where he usually stopped for refreshments.'

When he reached York his progress was slowed by crowds of punters and well wishers who had gathered to greet him. Powell took himself off to eat, drink and, strangely, to deliver some letters. He then slept for an hour and a half before slipping out of York in disguise to order to give the crowds the slip. He hurried back to London, but here was greeted by even larger crowds: 'There were not less than 3,000 persons on foot, on horseback, and in their carriages, who came with him from Highgate, accompanied with French horns.' Why this particular musical instrument was employed is as much a mystery as to why, twenty years later, he should have attempted to break his own record with such tragic consequences.

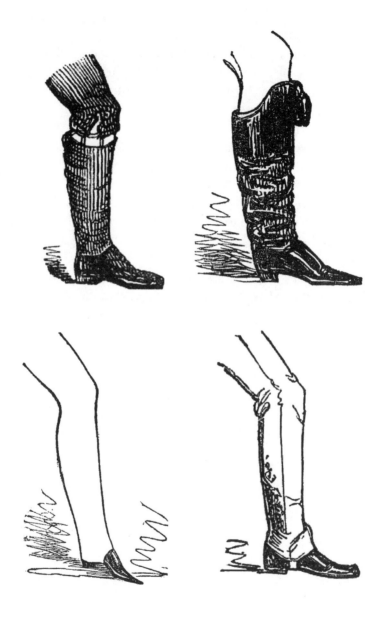

Footnote: Walking Boots

While certain Frenchmen in the 1780s expressed aston-ishment at the size of English women's feet (a conse-quence, it was concluded, of too much walking) *Punch* magazine received the best in the way of boots fifty years later. Both Ankle-jacks, favoured by butcher boys from East London, and Bluchers received short thrift – 'We don't like them.' Hessians were too old fashioned. Wellingtons, however, were judged perfect and might 'be walked about in not only as a protector of feet, but of the honour of the wearer'.

CAPTAIN ROBERT BARCLAY
*'The benefits of walking have been
recognised for many years'*

> Exercise on foot is allowed to be the most natural and
> perfect, as it employs every part of the body, and effectu-
> ally promotes the circulation of the blood through the
> arteries and veins.

So wrote the nineteenth century Walter Thom.
He added: 'The most obstinate diseases have been
frequently cured by perseverance in walking' and
helpfully provided a training programme for the
aspiring walker.

> Firstly purge the body with three doses of Gaulber salts.
> After four days of purging start training. Rise at 5.00
> a.m. and run a mile uphill at your fastest pace. Then
> walk six miles at a moderate pace and return for break-
> fast which should consist of mutton steaks under-done,
> with stale bread and old beer.

> After breakfast walk six miles at a moderate pace. On
> your return undertake a purging sweat which involves
> going to bed fully dressed and drinking strong liquor to
> induce the sweat. After dinner at 4.00 p.m. once again
> run uphill at your top pace and then walk six miles at a
> moderate pace. On your return eat a whole underdone
> chicken and then retire to bed. No more exercises should
> be done that day.

Captain Barclay completed his epic heel and toe walk in 1773 on a diet of small beer, tea and toast. *Gavan Tredoux (www.galton.org)*

This twenty-mile training regime, setting aside the dangers of food poisoning, was worth its weight in gold, literally. For this was the workout recommended by Robert Barclay, Captain, Royal Welsh Fusiliers, and the man who walked a thousand miles in a thousand days for a thousand guineas (around £35,000 in today's money).

Barclay, according to Walter Thom, who became Barclay's biographer, unveiled plans for his ambitious walk in 1809. Previous attempts on this record had failed after thirty days or less. Betting on Barclay's attempt was intense. There were rumours that the Prince of Wales had added his own purse and that this had raised the stakes up to an extravagant £100,000.

The event took place at Newmarket where Barclay was to walk a marked mile for forty one and a half days assisted by a back up team that included his servant William Cross and a bare-knuckle boxer, Big John Gully. At midnight on 1 June Barclay

A passion for sporting pedestrianism swept the country in the
eighteenth century. (*Punch*)

started walking. He wore a woollen overcoat, flannel
breeches, lambswool stockings and heeled, leather
shoes, and at night, suffered the additional weight
of a brace of pistols. The pistols, and the presence of

Big John Gully, were designed to prevent any attempt to sabotage the event.

At the outset he covered a mile in just under fifteen minutes, taking short, low steps to conserve his energy. At the end of each hour he ate or snatched a brief sleep. By the 999th mile he was still shuffling through each mile in around twenty-five minutes.

Barclay kept going on a high protein diet. He breakfasted at five in the morning on roast fowl, bread, butter, a pint of beer and two cups of tea (strange that after that lot he could walk at all). At midday he lunched on beef steak or mutton chops. For his six o'clock supper there was more mutton or beef together with a wine and porter while more fowl was served for supper at eleven o'clock. There were serious concerns that the attempt would fail when, arriving at the start of yet another mile, the Captain was observed to be still standing, but clearly asleep. The loyal William Cross struck his master violently across his back with a stick. Barclay awoke and staggered on.

The hero crossed the finishing line on 12 July at three in the afternoon to the sounds of cheering crowds and peeling church bells. He was thirty-two pounds lighter than when he started. Barclay immediately slept, was woken for a bowl of gruel, and then allowed a few more hours rest before taking a hot bath and returning to greet his fans. Five days later he rejoined his regiment, heading for the battlefields of Spain to fight the French. Captain Barclay died in 1854 not from war wounds, but from the stray kick of a horse.

As it turned out, the most famous walker of his time had been in training most of his life. Born in August 1809, he was the son of 'the Great Master of Ury', Robert Barclay senior, a Scottish Highlands laird and Westminster MP who kept one house in Ury and another in what was then the little country village of Brixton, just south of London. Robert Barclay senior regularly walked between his two residences, covering around fifty miles a day over ten days. Watching his own son take his first faltering steps must have been an anxious time for the father. The boy did not disappoint. By the age of fifteen Robert Barclay junior had completed his first timed walk, a distance of six miles in one hour. By the time he joined the Fusiliers, the young soldier thought nothing of walking forty miles to attend a dinner party. At twenty two he walked sixty miles a day over five, hot summer days between Ury and Boroughbridge in Yorkshire for a wager.

If Walter Thom is to be believed, Captain Barclay was a man of extraordinary stamina. Thom writes that when Barclay kept a pack of fox hounds, he frequently 'went from Ury to Turriff, a distance of fifty-one miles, where he arrived to breakfast'. Having attended to the pack and 'followed the hounds for a chase for twenty or twenty-five miles farther' Barclay would walk home. Thus twice weekly Barclay would walk between one hundred and thirty and one hundred and fifty miles, 'which he accomplished in about twenty-four hours.'

By now the soldier who could, and did, walk

more miles before breakfast than most could walk in a day was ready for a challenge. His early efforts were a struggle. Twice he attempted to walk ninety miles in twenty and a half hours and twice he was defeated by illness. His third attempt was along a specially marked mile on the road between York and Hull. The judges allowed a pace and a half at the turn of each mile and an additional ten paces to a nearby house for rest and refreshments. Captain Barclay finished with one hour and eight minutes to spare.

News of his efforts fuelled the public fever for sporting pedestrianism. It had been fired up by Foster Powell and by now one James West had found fame by running 126 miles in a day with the Berkeley hounds. A man called George Wilson had walked 1,000 miles in twenty days and, in 1789, Donald MacLeod walked from Inverness to London and back . . . and then back again, a distance of 1,680 miles. (A claim that Mr MacLeod was 100 years old at the time was not substantiated.) In July 1795 Thomas Miller of Cowford in Sussex set off to walk the thirty-six miles from the market house at Horsham to Westminster Bridge 'which he did in five hours and fifty minutes with apparent ease,' wrote Thom. Speed, he explained, was critical: 'Blewet from Crewkerne, Somerset for a small wager, undertook to go twenty-four miles in three hours. He did so at a rate of nine miles an hour.' A good purse was an added incentive: 'Mr Stevens went the twenty-five miles from St Albans to Finsbury Square in three

The Lady Globe Walker, Madam Florence, a noted pedestrienne in her time, walked from London to Brighton on a globe in June 1903.

hours, for a bet of four hundred and fifty guineas although it did involve some running.'

One of the more famous figures was Abraham Wood of Mildrew, Lancashire, a 'remarkably fine, tall well-made man . . . possessed of good WIND and good BOTTOM' wrote Thom. Although he was better known as a runner than a walker (he regularly ran without shoes), Wood was matched against Barclay at Newmarket in 1807. When Wood retired with foot injuries Barclay was accused of striking a secret deal with his adversary in order to share the 200 guineas that had been staked on the race. The controversy was forgotten when, two years later, Barclay managed his remarkable feat of 1,000 miles in 1,000 successive hours.

Barclay's achievement became the pedestrian's grail, for women as well as men. A female pedestrian, Mary Frith, was reported to have set out on a 500 mile walk from Maidstone in 1816 while a Miss Freeman from Strood walked thirty-five miles in seven hours and forty-nine minutes in 1823 at Chelsea: she was seven years old. The Barclay challenge was said to have been attempted by a Lancashire woman at Birkenhead in 1854 and, ten years later by an Australian, Margaret Douglas, in a London music hall. A Yorkshire woman, Emma Sharp successfully completed 1000 miles in 1000 hours at the Quarry Gap Hotel in Laisterdyke near Bradford. Dressed in a man's white waistcoat and laced boots she started in September 1864 and finished the following month watched by a crowd of 25,000 and guarded by a man with a loaded musket.

By now the sport of women walking was developing into a voyeuristic sideshow with women walking special planks in bars and saloon. That was until the redoubtable Ada Anderson took to the stage. The middle-aged former actress and singer had turned pedestrienne in the 1870s, following in the footfalls of another woman athlete, Bertha Von Hillern. The twenty-one year old German had pulled in large crowds for her walking competitions in America. Anderson set out to do the same, performing her walking feats in front of thousands. However she could crown herself champion walker of the world when at a Kings Lynn music hall in July 1878 she walked 1008 miles at a steady pace of a mile and a half an hour for 673 hours. She had broken the Barclay spell.

ALFRED WATKINS
'Mother Earth is good enough for you to walk on'

Alfred Watkins was a purposeful walker. Following a moment of revelation in 1921, he walked the byways of his home county, Herefordshire, convinced him that the kingdom had been covered once by an ancient network of straight tracks and that their marker points – earthworks, stones, beacon hills, and ancient ponds – were still in evidence.

His obituarist in the *Daily Express* of 9 April 1935 described him as a 'scholar, miller, archaeologist, naturalist, inventor, magistrate, County Councillor, politician and leader of public opinion'. His critics might have preferred a testimonial which included the words 'misguided fool' and even 'charlatan'.

The conventional history of tracks and byways suggests that highways evolved casually through need and necessity. Take the old Roman road from York through Scotch Corner to Bishop Auckland, now a dismal stretch of black tar and grit and the scene of death of the occasional unwary motorist. The corpulent Ben Jonson waddled along here on his way to Edinburgh in 1619, making his way past rumbling dray carts and crowds of cattle herded by their drovers. A thousand years before it was a minor monastic motorway, a route linking the abbeys of York, Easby and Riveaux. The friars passed milestones and trod roadstone laid down by the Roman builders who originally upgraded the muddy track linking their Essex barracks to those on Hadrian's Wall. Centuries

Alfred Watkins, right, developed radical ideas on how Britain's
byways had evolved. (Herefordshire Libraries)

before, Neolithic traders had trudged along the track
to trade their knapsacks of Norfolk flint with northern tribes. And who came before them? A migration
of Stone Age aurochs, their hoof prints dogged by
hungry, fur-clad hunters?

When in 1921 Watkins, the 'provincial visionary'
published his own ideas on how men and women
first found their way from A to B, his notions sparked
a controversy, which still rumbles on.

Watkins, the son of a successful brewer, invented
and patented designs for the first photographic expo-
sure meter. World sales followed after a testimonial
from H. G. Pointing, the photographer who accompanied Scott on his visit to Antarctica in 1910.
Watkins also campaigned against decimalisation,
proposing an alternative system based on eighths.

Communities along Welsh borders mapped by John Speede in 1610 were linked by ancient straight tracks, insisted Watkins.

He published a guide on bee-keeping, founded a historical society in his home city of Hereford and nearly died in an early road accident when his steam-driven Gardner-Serpollet crashed and overturned on a slippery road.

A summer's day in 1921, however, found him not in the seat of his Gardner-Serpollet, but sitting astride his brewery horse. He was looking out across the Welsh borderlands, gazing down on the web of tracks and trails which had been followed by meandering cattle, salt traders, coster mongers, legionnaires and monks. In an instant he had a very different vision of how they had come about. It was, he promised in *The Old Straight Track*, no more than any 'outdoor man, away on a cross-country tramp . . . lingering over his midday sandwich on the earthwork of a small hill-top camp' might recognise as he looked 'at the lay of the land'.

Watkins' envisioned an ancient network of straight tracks. They had, he concluded, been laid across the landscape by Stone Age men using sighting staves to devise direct routes across the countryside, 'like a fairy chain stretching from mountain peak to mountain peak'. He called the tracks leys because, when he consulted the maps, so many of the places along the routes had the word ley in the name.

The prehistoric surveyor or ley-man, he suggested, was the dod-man, the individual who carried 'two sighting staves as the Long Man of Wilmington, Sussex, does', to sight along the route. The dod-man aligned natural sighting points such as hills, notches on the horizon, river fords and wells, and added cairns of stones or marker stones to waymark the paths.

'In its full development, the old track was no mean achievement in surveying and engineering. Road-making was not part of its scheme, for the attitude seems to have been: "Mother earth is good enough for you to walk . . . on and we will pave a way through streams, soft places and ponds, our chief job is to make out the way." This the old ley-men did magnificently,' wrote Watkins. In time hamlets, burial places and temples were set along the routes. In time, too, astronomers, who could 'give seasonal information to tillers of the soil', became involved providing local alignments for occasions such as the midsummer and midwinter solstice, and the spring and autumn equinox.

The broad-shouldered, bespectacled and bearded Victorian who habitually wore Harris Tweed suits lined with fourteen pockets (stuffed with the usual paraphernalia of the antiquarian), followed up his visionary moment with practical observation and a study of place names. 'Words', he pointed out, 'were spoken in Britain for more centuries before they were written down.' Laying out local maps on his study table at 5 Harley Court just beyond the Cathedral Close in Hereford he noted significant places – burial mounds, boundary stones, beacons, old churches – and found, to his satisfaction, that alignments of a minimum of four such locations criss-crossed not only his home county, but the country as a whole. In places, at Glastonbury Tor for example, the number of alignments converging on the hill seemed to represent the Clapham Junction of an ancient world.

Watkins presented his theories to members of the local antiquarian club and, in 1925, published them in his best-known work, *The Old Straight Track*. Although The *New Statesman* described it as 'a first-rate piece of work' most academic journals ignored the book. One reviewer, 'reflecting on the instinct of the unregenerate walker to make for the nearest pub', experimented with ley line alignments using pubs alone. It was, he reported, an astounding success and completely debunked the ley line myth. Yet Watkins' leyline theory, with its blend of common sense and mysticism, had popular appeal.

Then in 1958, in a bizarre intervention, Aime Michel linked Watkins' ley lines with flying saucers, suggesting that ley lines were associated with the flight paths of Unidentified Flying Objects or UFOs. The industrious Alfred Watkins would have been astonished (and probably appalled) at the suggestions of a link between UFOs and ley lines. It was too much for the academics: 'There are no such things as 'leys' or 'ley lines', declared Dr Richard Muir firmly in the *Shell Guide to Reading the Landscape*. 'Books about leys ... sit snugly on the bookshelves between tomes of paganism, Atlantis, and those which prove God was a spaceman'. Appropriately enough the author of *The View Over Atlantis*, John Michell, hailed Watkins as 'an honest visionary who saw beyond the bounds of time.' By 1962 an international group of enthusiasts had formed the Ley Hunters Club and New Age theorists were pounding the paths of Britain as they speculated on the connection between Watkins' straight tracks and mystical sources of power. 'Orthodox archaeologists and other scientists have doused the New Age ideas with . . . bucketfuls of scorn,' warned Tom Williamson in *Dowsing – New Light on an Ancient Art*. 'But remembering how often orthodoxy has been proved wrong in the past, should we be so sure that our self-proclaimed guardians are right this time?'

So did Ben Jonson stride out on his mammoth walk to Edinburgh along an ancient, animal migration route, the alignment of a straight Neolithic track or a well-used UFO airstrip? All we can say with certainty is that he trod a path which has been trodden since time began.

CHAPTER 2

DEVOTED WALKERS

JOHN BUNYAN
'As I walked through the wilderness of this world . . .'

Two bishops from Cappadocia in Asia Minor (modern day Turkey) paid a visit to religious sites in Palestine in the third century and so began the business of the Christian pilgrimage. And business it was: the church by the thirteenth century had worked out a system of rewards for loyal service, based upon the pilgrimage. A dutiful canon, for example, could, after a year in residence, earn himself a three-week pilgrimage within England, according to documents in Hereford Cathedral's chained library.

In 312 a Roman empress who had converted to

A pair of feet, a miracle and a good shrine were all the pilgrim needed. (Arkitype)

Christianity made a pilgrimage to Jerusalem in her old age. She was Helen, the wife of the emperor Constantius Chlorus from whom she was separated in 292 after bearing Constantine the Great, who was proclaimed emperor by the Roman army at York in 306. Saint Helen, as she was to become, was supposed to have discovered the remains of Christ's cross buried on the Calvary hillside. No one knows how far the devout Roman physically walked in the Holy Land, but it was a great deal further than any empress before her. She certainly encouraged the cult of the pilgrim (which, according to the writings of Bishop Gregory of Nyssa, was already being abused by the end of the century).

Although the Holy Land was the pre-eminent pilgrimage site, there were, by the Middle Ages, plenty of religious sites to chose from in Europe: Fourvière, Le Puy and St Denis in France, Loretto, Assisi and, of course, Rome in Italy, Guadalupe and Montserrat in Spain, Cologne and Trier in Germany and Ensieldeln in Switzerland. In England the pilgrim might walk in an act of devotion to Canterbury or Walsingham founded in 1061. Many came hoping their prayers for a miraculous cure would be answered as *The Walsingham Ballad* told in 1496:

> Many seke ben here cured by our Lady's myghte
> Dede agayne revyved of this is no doubt
> Lame made hole and blynde restored to syghte
> Maryners vexed with tempest safe to porte brought
> Defe wonded and lunatyke that hyder have sought
> And also lepers here recovered have be
> By oure lady's grace of their infirmyte.

The correct procedure for visiting the shrine involved the pilgrim removing their shoes at the Slipper Chapel, a mile from the shrine, and proceeding on bare feet. In 1511 Henry VIII arrived here and duly removed his shoes for the final walk to kneel before the image of Our Lady. He was the last king of England to do so. Twenty-seven years later during his dissolution of the monasteries, he had the image of Our Lady brought to London and burned on a pyre.

You can't keep a good shrine down. In the past 400 years, places of pilgrimage have proliferated like tourist destinations in an air fare price war. Lourdes in France, dedicated in 1876, attracted 100,000 pilgrims in its first year. The following year there were a quarter of a million. The pilgrim could walk (or under new rules ride or cycle) to the Holy Mount in Austria, Santiago de Compostella in Spain, Medjugorje in Croatia, Fatima in Portugal, and San Giovanni Italy or Croagh Patrick, Lough Derg and Knock in Ireland.

The world's most famous pilgrim, however, never took a step in real life although his creator took many. This was the fictional Christian, hero of John Bunyan's *The Pilgrim's Progress*, an allegorical account of Christian's journey to the Celestial Country by way of Doubting Castle, ('they walked on their way; and the weather was comfortable to them'), the Delectable Mountains ('the way from the river was rough, and their feet tender by reasons of their travel'), Vanity Fair and the Slough of Despond. It was a book, wrote the walker poet Edward Thomas in *The Icknield Way*, 'full of the sense of roads'.

Bunyan was born in 1628, an inauspicious time in British religious history when dissent raged between Puritan, Catholic, Jesuit, Anglican, Presbyterian, Baptist, Congregationalist and Quaker alike. It was a bad time for the Bunyan family too. Bunyan's father's fortunes had slipped and he was now a tinker, a mender of kettles and pots. Bunyan followed the trade until, in 1644, he enlisted with the Parliamentarian forces to fight in the Civil War. After the war, and a narrow escape when a friend took his place and was killed instantly by a musket ball, Bunyan married and

Does my tum look big in this? A Victorian lady's walking outfit. (*Punch*)

found his faith. When a free church was founded at Bedford in 1650 Bunyan moved his family including his beloved, blind daughter Mary to be near the church. For the next thirty-five years he took up his prayer book and walking stick and supported his family as an itinerant, Nonconformist preacher. That is when he was not banged up for his beliefs, for the author of what would become the third best selling book in the world was regularly jailed for his seditious preaching.

Pilgrims Progress begins: 'As I walked through the wilderness of this world I lighted on a certain place where was a den and laid me down in that place to sleep.' Bunyan penned the words, not after some inspiring hike through the Bedfordshire countryside, but while incarcerated in Bedford gaol. It was in his mind's eye that he sent the good Christian wandering the marshy mere near Shalford (said to have been the inspiration for the Slough of Despond), visited Shalford Fair (the supposed model for Vanity Fair) or took his rest at Horn Hatch cottage where he was believed to have lived. He took Christian through the three stages of the journey, the stages identified by the anthropologist Arnold van Gennys as separation, transition (or the liminal from the Latin, *limen* or threshold phase) to incorporation, where the passage of the pilgrim is finally consummated.

Bunyan died in August 1688 after being caught in a downpour and catching a fever on his way to London. He was buried in the dissenters' graveyard at Bunhill Fields. While poverty compelled Bunyan to walk, he earns his place here as an inspiration to other walkers, to men like Pastor Carl Philip Moritz who, a century later, was setting out on foot along the London road.

Footnote: What Walkers Wear

Pilgrims did not abandon their dress sense and slip on a hair shirt when they took to the trail. Although some of the fourteenth century pilgrims to Limoges in France were inclined to divest themselves of all clothing as they neared their destination, most pilgrim walkers followed the tradition described by Sir Walter Raleigh in His Pilgrimage.

Give me my scallop shell of quiet

My staff of faith to walk upon
My scrip of joy, immortal diet;
My bottle of salvation;
My gown of glory, hopes true gage
And thus I'll take my pilgrimage.

The scrip was a leather pouch containing cash and hung around the shoulder of the sclavein, a long sleeved, coarse tunic sometimes embroidered with a cross and held in with a large leather belt. A wide-brimmed hat was traditional and a useful place from which to hang the little lead symbols issued by each shrine: the scallop or cockle shell of Santiago, the Annunciation token at Walsingham, St Michael weighing souls at the Last Judgement for Mont Saint-Michel, the palm of Jericho from Jerusalem, and from Canterbury another scallop shell.

As for the pilgrim's 'staff of faith', this was no mere medieval walking pole. With two legs and a staff the pilgrim was symbolically supported by the Trinity. For the poet Samuel Coleridge a staff was purely practical. He stole the household broom stick amid much protest from his family. Coleridge also held some curious views on what constituted essential attire for the walker: along with a shirt, a cravat and two pairs of stockings, he liked to take his night cap. Head gear is an indispensable item of any walker's wardrobe and Robert Louis Stevenson chose to pack not only his flannel shirt ('of an agreeable dark hue which the satirical call black'), a light tweed coat made by a good English tailor, ready-made cheap linen trousers, leather gaiters, and a smoking cap 'of Indian work the gold lace pitifully frayed and tarnished.'

PASTOR MORITZ
'The short English miles are delightful for walking'

The walker was an object of scorn and derision in eighteenth century England. That at least was the experience of Pastor Carl Philip Moritz, an earnest German who, in 1782, set off on foot from London to walk to the Peak District.

It may be that Moritz walked simply because he hated coach travel. 'The poorest Englishman one sees, is prouder and better pleased to expose himself to the danger of having his neck broken on the outside of a stage (coach), than to walk any considerable distance, though he might walk ever so much at his ease,' observed Moritz. His opinion was coloured by his own, mostly unfortunate, experiences of travelling on four wheels. On a coach journey to London, for example, he was obliged to share his carriage with three farmers who either slept, 'their faces, bloated and discoloured by their copious use of ale and brandy', or else talked shop or rather sheep, 'the first and last topic of their conversation'. On another tedious coach ride, this time from Oxford to Birmingham 'all that was to be seen between the two places was entirely lost to me, for I was again mewed up in a post-coach, and driven along with such velocity from one place to another, that I seemed to myself as doing nothing less than travelling.' Naturally the pastor preferred to walk. He walked not 'out of absolute poverty, but with a view of becoming better acquainted with men and manners'. But why, he wondered, did not more Englishmen do the same? A fellow traveller explained: 'We are too rich, too lazy, and too proud'.

Carl Moritz spent seven weeks in England, walking first to Richmond, Windsor and Oxford, and then from Birmingham through Sutton, Lichfield and Burton to Derby and the Peak District before returning to London, again frequently on foot. At the start of his outward journey he suffered the doubts familiar to anyone embarking on the first stage of a long walk. 'I have already . . . experienced so many inconveniences as a traveller on foot, that I am at some loss to determine whether or no I shall go on with my journey in the same manner.'

At first he persevered, but his progress was made more difficult by the generally hostile reception

With cap, map and compass, a group of walkers in the 1970s.
(*YHA*)

he received. Passing through one village he hears
a succession of old women exclaiming 'Good God!'
as he passes. He concludes that a traveller on foot
is considered as 'a sort of wild man or out-of-the
way being, who is stared at, pitied, suspected, and
shunned by everybody that meets him'.

In spite of the difficulties, Moritz's letters, later
translated and published in 1795 as *Travels, chiefly
on foot, through several parts of England in 1782*,
reveal some of the singular delights of a long walk.
For example, there are the English milestones which
'give me much pleasure . . . telling me how far I
had already gone, and by assuring me that I was
on the right road.' At Windsor he is alarmed by
the steel traps and spring guns lying in wait for the

Carl Philip Moritz experienced nothing but trouble in his encounters with English landladies. *(Punch)*

unwary country walker, but at Nettlebed church in Oxfordshire he is cheered by the graveyard humour of the memorial inscriptions:

Physicians were in vain;
God knew the best;
So here I rest'

And on a marble monument:

The same good sense which qualified him for every public employment
Taught him to spend his life here in retirement.

Passing the night at the Mitre in Oxford he toler-

Ramblers in Derbyshire in the 1930s. Carl Philip Moritz also enjoyed the barren mountains and lofty rocks of the Peak District. (YHA)

ates a foolish clergyman called Clerk 'who seemed ambitious to pass for a great wit, . . . by telling us again and again, that he should still be at least a Clerk, even though he should never become a clergyman'.

Moritz swims 'in the cool tide of the Thames' and is joined by some lively apprentice boys who, 'with the greatest expedition, threw off their clothes and leathern aprons, and plunged themselves, head foremost, into the water, where they opposed the tide with their sinewy arms'.

When he reaches Castleton in the high Peaks of Derbyshire, twenty miles from Matlock, he records the dramatic change of scenery from the green meadows and pleasant hills of Windsor and Richmond to the 'barren mountains and lofty rocks'. He notes how the fields and pasture lands were 'fenced with a wall of grey stone; and of this very same stone, . . . all the houses are built in a very uniform and patriarchal manner, inasmuch as the rough stones are almost without any preparation placed one upon another.' He wonders at the Eldon Hole, 'of such a monstrous depth' and into which some person once threw a goose, 'which appeared again at two miles' distance . . . quite stripped of its feathers'.

The London road to Oxford he judges 'a charming fine broad road'; Birmingham, he says, is pronounced 'by the common people Brummidgeham'; Nottingham he declares to be 'one of the best, and is undoubtedly the cleanest' towns outside of London, while Lichfield is 'an old-fashioned town with narrow dirty streets, where for the first time I saw round panes of glass in the windows', a reference to the glazier's use of cheap off cuts or 'bull's eye' panes. At Burton he hits a low point finding it 'odious and almost insupportable' for the residents' 'strongly-marked contemptuous treatment of a stranger, who was travelling through their country'.

Walking at an average speed of four 'English miles' an hour he records, 'it is a pleasing exchange to find that in two hours I can walk eight miles: the short English miles are delightful for walking'. He has brushed up on his English, for 'the more I spoke (English), the more attention and regard I met with'. This fluency enables him to correct an odd urban myth relayed to him by the innkeeper of The Bear near Derby, that Germans have a singular talent for playing the French horn. 'I removed this error.'

Try as he might, however, he cannot reverse the apparently universal view amongst landladies and inn-keepers that those who walk are essentially low-lifers. Landlords slam doors in his face, publicans show him to the kitchen rather than the parlour for his meals, and landladies force him to share a room with drunkards or show him rooms 'that much resembled a prison for malefactors'.

Moritz is travelling with his beloved copy of Milton's *Paradise Lost* (he avoids reading it by the wayside after being jeered at by a passing coach of travellers), some maps, a pocket book and money enough to pay his way. It is just as well: 'If they considered me but as a beggar . . . they suffered me to pay like a gentleman'. Occasionally he takes his revenge. When a particularly sour and unhelpful maid looks for a tip and confronts him with a 'pray remember the chambermaid' he tells her: '"Yes, yes. I shall long remember your most ill-mannered behaviour and shameful incivility"; and so I gave her nothing'.

Fifteen years later a John Feltham read about Moritz's experiences and 'feeling the truth of these remarks' set out with a friend to walk from Salisbury to Liverpool in order to 'retrieve our characters'. Covering more than fifty miles a day for the first seven days ('expenses £2 8 10') and returning to Salisbury in eight days, after paying a visit to the Isle of Man, Feltham and his friend walked 198 miles. He failed to record whether they suffered the same abuse as Moritz simply adding at the end of his account: 'The country appeared everywhere rich and beautiful'.

And in spite of England's inhospitality our patient pastor seems to have returned to Germany a happy man: 'I must confess that all this journey has seemed but as it were one continued walk for pleasure'.

REV'DS BINGLEY, WILLIAMS AND WARNER
'My mode of travelling was chiefly on foot'

Poor Pastor Moritz was but one of a congregation of clerics who were, by now, keen to take a long walk. Fifteen years after Moritz's troublesome encounters with surly hoteliers and landladies, three clergymen were packing their bags and heading for the Welsh hills: the Rev'd W. Bingley and his friends the Rev'd Mr Williams, and the Rev'd Richard Warner.

Bingley, through the pages of his *In North Wales* (1814) advised fellow pedestrians to take a guide (he rarely did so), to make an early start (around five or six o'clock in the morning), and to stop frequently to admire the scenery. Walking in Wales meant walking amongst foreigners, many of whom had

The early 1800s
saw a congregation
of clerics heading
for the hills on foot.

no English: but the tourist who might occasionally be perplexed by the reply 'Dim Saesnag' (no English) to a question might 'proceed through a great part of Wales without being inconvenienced by a want of knowledge of the native language.' Leaving aside the phrase book, the walker, nevertheless, should take a sufficient supply of food: Bingley carried his in an eighteenth-century version of the bum-bag, a basket strapped around his waist. A spiked stick and hob nailed boots were useful but 'if a person is in good health and spirits, he will find that he can do without either.'

Rev'd Warner was also anxious to be properly equipped for his walk. John Feltham who had undertaken his walk to test Pastor Moritz's theories, knew the clergyman. In his *A Tour through the Island of Man* in 1797 and 1798 he described Warner as wearing 'a Spencer fitted up with a large sportsman's pocket to carry his linen, etc.; and Mr. C., who accompanied him, had sidepockets annexed to his coat'. Unfortunately, noted Feltham, 'neither answered perfectly their wishes'. Warner had expressed some interest in a party whom they met on the way equipped with 'a handsome leather bag covered with net-work . . . suspended from the shoulder, and hung under the left arm like a shooting bag'. Apparently it proved 'no inelegant addition'. However they were united in their scorn for another party who drove a pony, which 'carried their portmanteau before them'. The beast turned out to be 'more plague than profit' and the pony was sold.

Thus equipped, but with the added weight of notebooks and pencils, the three men of God struck out for the Welsh hills, Warner in 1797, Bingley and Williams in 1798. Bingley, then resident in Cambridge, had, he said, made 'several tours through nearly all the romantic parts of the North of England' ('the Lakes of the north' had been a particular disappointment), but North Wales was quite perfect for 'the traveller of taste, the naturalist and the antiquary' especially in the 'romantic country of North Wales, namely Denbighshire, Caernarvonshire, Meironethshire and Anglesea'.

During the three months of his 'College avocations' Bingley met up with Williams, 'a clergyman of the neighbourhood' who accompanied him on several of their rambles. 'My mode of travelling was chiefly on foot, but sometimes I took horses, and at other times proceeded in carriages,' he wrote. The former mode of travel, however, 'notwithstanding all the objections that have been made against it, will I am confident, upon the whole, be found most useful, if health and strength are wanting'. For the pedestrian, explained the patient Bingley, could not only 'examine the countryside as he goes along' but could also 'strike out of the road, amongst mountains and morasses, in a manner completely independent'.

Thus it was that Bingley and Williams came to make what was to be the first recorded ascent of the eastern side of Clogwyn du'r Arddu. Bingley was a keen botanist and had already ascended Penmaen Mawr in search of what the Welsh called 'Pren

Lemwn' or the lemon tree. He was disappointed to discover it was 'nothing more than Crataegus aria of Linnaeus'. While the two men were searching for plants, they found themselves edging inexorably up the mountain. 'We began our laborious task without once reflecting on the many dangers that might attend it.' An hour and a half later they found themselves on top of 'this dreadful precipice' having collected several plants. (Rev'd Warner would prove wimpish by comparison, recording that he was 'struck dumb with terror' on Cader Idris although his guide skipped along with the agility of a goat). Bingley and Williams scaled Snowdon and later made a fourteen hour hike along the classic tramp from Llanberris to Cwm Idwal taking in Tryfan, Glyder Fach and Glyder Fawr before returning to Llanberris. At Tryfan, Bingley paused to admire the scenery: 'The mountain grandeur of the vale was broken by the wooded foreground; and the water of one of the lakes, from the rays of the sun, which shone obliquely upon it, glittered through the dark foliage of the trees'.

Continuing their walking tour they reached Beddgelert where Bingley relates the tragic tale of 'Bedd Cilhart'. Cilhart or Gelert was the loyal greyhound slain by his master, Llewellyn the Great. When Llewellyn returned from hunting, he found the hound covered in blood outside the nursery. Behind Bedd Cilhart the baby's cradle lay overturned, 'the ground flowing with blood'. Llewellyn drew his sword and slew the dog. Too late did he discover the babe safe and well and lying by the body of a wolf. Realising that his hound had killed the wolf and saved the child, the distraught Llewellyn erected a tomb over the dog's grave. From this story, says Bingley, was derived the common Welsh proverb: 'I repent as much as the man who slew his greyhound'. David Pritchard, the manager of the Goat Hotel who had promoted and embellished the tale to encourage local tourism presumably remained unrepentant.

Sometimes Bingley found the tramp something of a trudge: 'I had heard much in praise of the walk betwixt Bangor and Caernarvon, but I found very little to amuse me,' he noted with disappointment. Then he passed the fourth mile stone and was greeted by the view across the Menai Straits: it was 'one of the most exquisite landscapes the eye ever beheld.' Bingley walked 'entirely *round* the country' and 'not satisfied with this single journey I returned in North Wales, in the year 1801, and resided there four months more.'

Rev'd Warner in his walking accounts, *Walks through Wales* (1798) and *A Second Walk through Wales* (1799), gave a more impersonal account. In 1797 on his 462 mile tramp through the country he encountered impoverished lead miners in Denbighshire and concluded: 'the nature of their employment is obviously unwholesome. Their appearance denotes an imperfect state of health, it being commonly pale, wan and weakley'. He is fascinated to find men fishing with coracles beneath an old stone bridge at Machynlleth. 'Intended to carry only one person each, they are not more than five feet long, and four broad, rounded at the corners, and constructed of wickerwork; and are consequently sufficiently light to be conveyed on the back of the fishermen to his home, when the labour of the day is concluded.'

Making his way home through Monmouthshire – he lived in Bath – he was 'frequently retarded by droves of black cattle from Pem and Cwm travelling towards the Passage to be transported across the Severn and driven towards the markets of Bristol and the other large towns of Somerset, Glos and Wilts.'

In August and September of the same year Warner is away again, this time walking a respectable 763 miles to research his *A Second Walk Through Wales*. Passing through Caerleon he pauses to admire its Roman remains, but is troubled by the local inhabitants' 'want of common curiosity' about their heritage. He recounted the story of a developer whose workmen unearthed 'a mass of fragments of ancient masonry' while digging the foundations for a large warehouse. 'He went to the excavation, looked at the remains with perfect indifference, and coolly observing that "thes'em sort of things had nothing to do with his coal speculation," ordered the workmen to cover them up', reported the outraged cleric.

While Warner's walking observations reflect a passion for antiquities, like Bingley, he was not insensible to a good yarn. Before leaving Caerleon he reported on the unfortunate Mrs Williams, who, returning from a neighbour's house at night across a wooden planked bridge over the Usk, fell through on 'a faithless board' and was swept away straddled across her home-made raft, her candle still alight. Mrs Williams was 'on the point of encountering the turbulent waves of the Bristol Channel', when the master of a fishing-boat, returning from his nightly toils, discovered the floating lady of the night. She was rescued and returned safely to the shore.

In the years to come Warner employed his anecdotal skills once more when he wrote a satire on life in fashionable Bath. It failed to endear him to the characters he described. *A Walk Through Wales*, however, attracted positive reviews and the attention of a poet with a passion for walking, William Wordsworth. Wordsworth travelled to Bath in the spring of 1798 to meet Rev'd Warner. The clergyman doubtless dined out on the story of this encounter for years to come, not least because the famous poet was soon to follow the very route through Wales which Warner had pioneered.

FRANCIS KILVERT
'You're a splendid walker, Sir'

In the autumn of 1865 Mr Smith, a Newport clerk, arrived at Machynlleth in mid Wales determined to walk over Cader Idris. He offered a local guide two shillings and sixpence to take him across the mountain, but, the standard fee being five shillings up and ten shillings for the whole journey, the offer was refused. Moreover the guide warned Mr Smith against going at all: the weather was turning and darkness was falling. The clerk would not, or could not postpone his plan and, asking to be put on the right road, walked off in the gathering gloom along the Dolgellau road towards Cader Idris. He would not be seen alive again, despite a search of the mountain. The following spring a walker came across his gruesome remains.

The Victorian clergyman, Rev'd Francis Kilvert, undertaking the same walk just over six years later, noted in his diary: 'The foxes and ravens had eaten him. His eyes were gone. His teeth dashed out by the fall and lay scattered about the mountain. His head was bent double and crushed into his chest so that his neck was broken. The only piece of flesh remaining on the bone was where the coat buttoned over the chest. One leg was gone and one boot. The body must have fallen 440 yards.' Although Kilvert was not a wealthy man, he sensibly chose to employ a guide, 'Old Pugh', the same man who had helped recover the remains of Mr Smith. (Almost seventy years before Rev'd Bingley advocated: 'The persons who wish to ascend Cader Idris from Dolgelley will do well to select Richard Pugh, junior, to accompany them.')

Another gentleman in the tradition of striding clerics, Francis Kilvert regularly walked the hills of his parishes. 'In April 1870 I had the satisfaction of managing to walk from Hay to Clyro by the fields without meeting a single person, always a great triumph to me and a subject for warm self congratulations for I have a special dislike to meeting people, and a peculiar liking for a deserted road,' he recorded in his diary. And again in September: 'at 10.45 started across the fields to walk to Capel y Ffin.' Aside from his trip to North Wales Kilvert could not afford to go on walking tours and much of his tramping around the districts of Chippenham in Wiltshire and Clyro on the Welsh borders was confined to what he called 'villaging about'. ('Villaging about to Mrs Jones at the Infant School, Jo Phillips and Margaret Griffith, who told me that in the old-fashioned farmhouses a steen of butter and something particularly good was always kept till March and not touched because March was reckoned a very severe month.' Friday 24 February 1871.)

Kilvert was one of six children of his curiously named mother, Thermuthis Coleman, and her husband, the Rev'd Robert Francis Kilvert, rector of Hardenhuish, north of Chippenham in Wiltshire and later of the neighbouring parish of Langley Burrell Without. He followed his father into the Church, served as curate for a time and for seven years, from 1865, was the impoverished curate of Clyro, the little Radnorshire parish which lay in the pretty Wye valley a few miles west of Hay-on-Wye. He spent another four years as his father's curate in Wiltshire before taking on the living at St Harmon in north Radnorshire. A year later, in 1877, the living at Bredwardine, around five miles east of Hay in Herefordshire, became vacant. Kilvert was appointed the vicar. A month after his marriage to Elizabeth Anne Rowland, Kilvert died sud-

The diarist and cleric Francis Kilvert. (Kilvert Society)

denly of peritonitis and was buried at Bredwardine. Elizabeth, who never remarried, is thought to have destroyed most of Kilvert's diaries, possibly because of his account of their courtship: the clergyman was a frank diarist. Later, a niece destroyed all but three of the remaining notebooks. These three diaries, the vestiges of a short but passionate life, portray the life of a young clergyman with a spring in his step, an eye for a pretty face and a passion for walking:

> 'Started at noon to walk to Newchurch. This old field path is quite new to me. Just above the kiln I saw and gathered the first red campion. Luxuriantly large cowslips grew on the bank and marsh buttercups in the ditch.'

Kilvert reached Newchurch school where 'pretty

Emmeline in a russet brown stuff dress and her long curls was keeping school bravely' (he is later to mourn her premature death) and plants a kiss on the cheek of a young pupil, Janet, for doing her sums. 'Shall I confess that I have travelled ten miles today over the hills for a kiss.'

On 27 April 1870 he fetches out his old Swiss haversack, crams it with 'night necessaries' and, making a brown paper parcel of his dress coat, starts out after lunch for Whitney Rectory, 'walking with my pack slung over my shoulders by the fields to Hay'.

Kilvert's constant walking was the consequence of what he called his lack of prospects. And often as he walks he reflects on the fickle nature of love: 'I have been in a fever all day about Daisy, restless and miserable with uncertainty'. When he broaches the subject of marriage to a prospective father-in-law, Major Thomas of Llanthomas, the Major enquires about his prospects. Receiving the ever optimistic reply the Major 'shook his head over them'. Later Kilvert receives a letter from the Thomas household bidding him to 'give up all thoughts and hope of Daisy'. The young clergyman loses neither heart nor wit. 'This evening being May Eve I ought to have put some birch and wittan (mountain ash) over the door to keep out the old witch,' he writes admitting that he was too lazy to fetch the branches. He hopes the old witch will not come in during the night, but the young witches, he declares, 'are welcome'.

His trip to North Wales in June 1871 presented him with the opportunity for a long walk and a little

The Rev'd Francis Kilvert was never happier than when 'villaging about' in his Welsh border parishes.

flirtation – 'I was very much struck and taken with the waitress at the Golden Lion. She said her name was Jane Williams and that her home was at Bettws y Coed. She was a beautiful girl with blue eyes, eyes singularly lovely, the sweetest saddest most weary and most patient eyes I ever saw.'

The next morning 'as we sloped up the mountain side we had beautiful views of the Harlech Mountain opposite, blue Cardigan Bay and dim Snowdon,' he recalled. Then the weather breaks and Kilvert finds the mountain 'an awful place in a storm. I thought of Moses on Sinai'. Cader Idris under snow and a blue

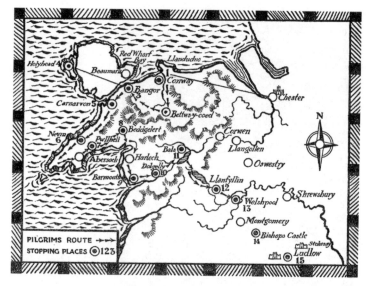

Map showing the pilgrims' route through North Wales with numbered stopping places. Locations shown include Holyhead, Red Wharf Bay, Llandudno, Beaumaris, Conway, Bangor, Chester, Carnarvon, Bettws-y-coed, Nevin, Beddgelert, Corwen, Pwllheli, Bala, Llangollen, Oswestry, Abersoch, Harlech, Dolgelly, Barmouth, Llanfyllin, Shrewsbury, Welshpool, Montgomery, Bishops Castle, Stokesay, Ludlow.

PILGRIMS ROUTE →→→
STOPPING PLACES ⊙123

1871 saw Kilvert tackling some of the classic walks in North Wales.

sky has an alpine beauty, but in foul weather the little mountain can be as treacherous as its taller sister, Snowdon. As cloud, rain and swirling mists descend on Kilvert and his guide Pugh, the pair are forced to shelter in a bothy.

Kilvert worried that they would be marooned for the night, an unenviable situation for as legend has it, any one who spends a night on top of Cader Idris will be found the next day either 'dead, or a madman or a poet gifted with the highest degree of inspiration'. Old Pugh adds to the clergyman's discomfort reporting with confidence that the fairies used to dance here. But Old Pugh knows his stuff. Having thoroughly frightened the priest, he leads him, as dark descends, safely back down the mountain to their hotel in Dolgellau. 'You're a splendid walker, Sir,' Pugh tells Kilvert, a compliment which promptly earns the wily old guide a brandy.

CANON COOPER
'The man who walks is the man who is well'

Canon Cooper hurried the final bars of the Nunc Dimitis on Sunday evensong at St Oswalds for he was anxious to be on the road to London before dark. As he ushered the last parishioner out of the porch of the parish church at Filey in Yorkshire he timed his preparations for departure. He collected his satchel and checked its contents – spare shirt and socks, money deposited in three different pockets plus a bank note sewn 'in the waistband of my unmentionables'. A quarter of an hour later he strode forth with his walking stick.

Since he was required to return to conduct Matins at St Oswalds the following Sunday, and since his destination, the Bank of England, was 200 miles away, he kept up a good pace. He was minded by neither the weather nor the dark for 'the open air to my mind is always enjoyable,' the parson would record in his book, *With Knapsack and Notebook*.

Canon Arthur Neville Cooper was dubbed the Walking Parson, although he was but one of a virtual choir of pedestrian clegyman. (Stephen Graham in *The Gentle Art of Tramping*, published in 1925, men-

Cannon Cooper who always carried a ten pound note in his 'unmentionables' when walking. (Filey Museum)

tions the tramping vicar of Southbourne who regularly published his impressions of walking in Spain in the parish magazine). Cooper was a missionary in the domestic sense, his mission being to open up the world of walking to the humbler person. Morris Marples in *Shanks's Pony* judged him 'essentially a plain, straightforward man . . . whose only unusual characteristics were his queer passion for making long, solitary walking tours and his belief that it was his duty to induce others to make them too.' Canon Cooper particularly recommended walking to men like himself, men who were condemned to live their lives in smart clothes dining regularly with serviettes and finger glasses. Walking, he declared, was the best way of dispelling one's cares and worries.

Canon Cooper was born in Windsor at the centre point of the nineteenth century. He began his working life as a clerk at Somerset House in London making the daily journey from home to work, four miles and back, on foot to save the bus fare. At twenty-five he joined the Church of England and served as a curate at Chester-le-Street before moving to St Oswalds at Filey in 1880. Here he stayed, marrying a local girl, Maud Nicholson, in 1891, until his death in 1943 at the age of ninety-three.

He was thirty-six and still a batchelor when he embarked on his walk from Filey to the Bank of England in London. The walk was a personal test, a trial run for a six week, 740 mile walk from Filey to Rome which he planned to begin on Easter Day in 1887, the following year. Cooper felt compelled to undertake the walk after reading John Ruskin's views on walking: the philanthropic Victorian had declared in *Stones of Venice* that the joys of walking were at an end. They were not, insisted the Canon, pointing out to his readers that George V, taken on a walking tour by his tutor, Mr Tarver, had learned more from his walk than from his lesson books. Walking was an improving exercise: cycling, thought Cooper, was not. He feared that an excess of cycling might lead to an eventual loss of energy in the walking limbs. (His reservations about the bicycle were shared by another inveterate walker and occasional cyclist, W.H. Hudson who reported in *Afoot in England* that birds were insensible to the

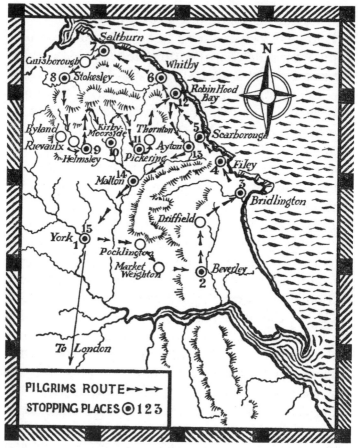

In 1886 Canon Cooper set out for London on foot from his parish at Filey in Yorkshire.

dangers of the bicycle wheel and were frequently injured trying to fly across the cyclist's path.)

The real reason most people preferred the bicycle, horse or carriage to their own two feet was an innate fear of getting wet feet. He claimed to have tempted

Providence in a hundred ways resting on damp grass and sleeping in wet socks, without taking harm (his patent method of setting off with washed socks each morning was to sluice them in soap and water the night before, and dry them on his feet overnight). In extreme situations he advocated that the wet walker pour a dose of whisky into his shoes to provide relief against the ordeal of wet feet.

Canon Cooper conducted himself well on his pioneering walk to London, reaching the Bank just before it closed at two o'clock: he had a dividend to collect. He had hoped to lose a little weight but found he weighed as much to the ounce as when he had started. He did, however, attract the attention of the press and in the months before his departure to Rome was gratified to have received letters 'from pedestrians of both sex'.

On Easter morning, 11 April 1887 Cooper waved farewell to his parishioners and headed off from Filey towards Rome, by way of the rather less romantic Bridlington. He was well prepared. He wore a black, trilby-like hat, a dark suit jacket smartly buttoned up over his knickerbockers, puttees and black leather shoes. In his leather gloves he carried his favourite blackthorn walking stick, and his satchel, slung across his shoulder, containing his brush and shaving kit. Like any walker, he slipped in a few nonessential items: a pocket edition of Horace's *Odes*, a pair of slippers and a white tie for Sundays (like his Lord and Maker, Cannon Cooper treated Sunday as a day of rest). His spare vest and pants he left behind in the

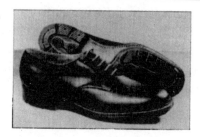
rectory dressing room (blushing at the thought that he would manage by washing his unmentionables only once a fortnight.) He carried neither raincoat nor umbrella.

Cooper planned a route through Antwerp, Strasbourg, Basle, St Gothard Pass, Milan, Bologna, Leghorn and Civita Vecchia, a distance of 800 miles as the crow flies. Experience taught him to average forty miles a day – twenty-five miles on the first – and not to exceed 150 miles in a week. By increasing his weekly average to 180 miles he expected to

Cooper doubted the benefits
of cycling which, he thought,
sapped the energy of the legs.
(Eve Huskins)

reach Rome in five weeks. Every walking morning
he spoke his Matins and every evening his Evensong.
In between he mentally composed letters home or
learned another Horace Ode. There were minor irri-
tations to contend with. He arrived at one lodging
house wet through and was obliged to take supper
dressed in two of his landlady's skirts. And he lost
his way in Pavia, experiencing the intense disappointment of the walker who must retrace his steps
to regain the route.

Yet he reached Rome, still with change in his
pocket from his budget of £30, and spied the dome
of St Peter's. He was so moved by the vision of the
church that, he confessed, had he been walking with
a companion he would have been too choked up to
speak. The lack of a companion was deliberate. After

his Rome journey, and for the next thirty-three years Canon Cooper went on to criss cross Europe, walking to Venice and Vienna, to Barcelona and Berlin, to Monte Carlo and Madrid always on foot and always alone. Not that Cooper walked an empty road. The byways of Europe were busy with men, and women and children, down on their luck and looking for work. Cooper admired their fortitude. On one occasion he encountered a tramp who had returned from some failed enterprise in America and is walking from London to Speeton living on his savings of half a crown (15 pence) by sleeping rough, eating only bread and cheese and drinking nothing but pump water. When the Canon takes to the road he is, he says, besieged by reporters and admires. Nobody pays attention to the tramp: 'no one specially wants to see a man without a penny in his pockets'.

By 1920 when the Walking Parson finally removed his walking shoes, he had walked most of the Britain, written a small library of walking books including *The Tramps of a Walking Parson* (1902) *With Knapsack and Notebook* (1906) and *Walking as Education* (1910), and given instructive interviews to the press. A seasoned walker, he told one reporter, needed only a pair of strong legs and enough money for bed and board. 'The very exercise is a joy to me and the open air is my elixir of life.'

CHAPTER 3

POETS IN MOTION

'THREE PERSONS AND ONE SOUL'

Finding the perfect walking companion is never easy. A couple who have been lovers for a lifetime can suddenly discover a disturbing incompatibility on the hills. The best of friends can fall out over one's preference to reach the destination quickly and the other's desire to savour the journey.

These were reasons enough for Samuel Coleridge to quit the company of his old friends, William and Dorothy Wordsworth, during their tour of Scotland in 1803. 'I am enjoying myself having Nature with solitude and liberty,' he insisted as he set off on what turned out to be his final long tramp. Yet only six years earlier, and in the same company, Coleridge had enjoyed the most creative walk of his life. The three had set off along the North Somerset coast one chill November morning in 1797 as 'three persons and one soul,' he declared.

On the face of it the three were as compatible as a pony, a horse and a donkey, each able to walk, but each in their own inimitable fashion. Dorothy, despite the constrictions of a long skirt, was solid and determined, a walker who would travel for hours without complaint as she recorded before they parted company with Coleridge in 1803. 'I can always walk over a moor with a light foot: I am . . . better satisfied with myself for being able to find enjoyment in what unfortunately to many persons is either dismal or insipid.' Her brother, always in a state of motion, according to their friend Thomas de Quincey, seemed to sail along, often deep in thought. He had 'an air somewhat stately and Quixotic,' wrote another friend William Hazlitt. 'Mr Wordsworth is often silent, indolent and reserved . . . although he has a peculiar sweetness in his smile and great depth and manliness and a rugged harmony.' Coleridge, his hair tumbling down to his shoulders, had difficulty holding a straight line. Thomas Carlyle described him, perhaps unkindly, as 'short, rotund and relaxed. He never straightens his knee-joint. He stoops with his fat, ill-shapen shoulders, and in walking does not tread, but shovel and slide.' Worse still Coleridge possessed a habit which would jeopardise any walking trip: he would, like a wayward spaniel, constantly cross the path of his companions.

Hazlitt would observe: 'he continually crossed me on the way by shifting from one side of the footpath to the other. This struck me as an odd movement; but I did not at the time connect it with any instability of purpose or involuntary charge of principles, as I have done since. He seemed unable to keep in a straight line'.

Nevertheless their two day walk was a triumph. It provided Coleridge with the opening lines for his epic poem, 'The Rime of the Ancient Mariner'; it transformed the literary world of the seventeenth century; and it helped to turn all three into eighteenth century celebrities. The trio meandered over Somerset's Quantock Hills, with its views over the grassy cliffs of the racing tides of the Bristol Channel and the hills of Wales beyond.

Distance was no obstacle. Coleridge regularly walked eight to twelve miles and back from his home at Nether Stowey to preach at the Unitarian chapels in Bridgwater and Taunton. And before William and Dorothy moved to be nearer their friend, William thought nothing of walking 40 miles to visit.

On this walk the three were strapped for cash and they set out determined to trade poems for a night's lodging – poetic passion rather than a backpacker's forethought ruled their preparations. From Watchet they walked on through Minehead, Lynton and back to the Wordsworths' home at Alfoxden. In the course of the 35 miles, the walkers concluded that eighteenth century poetry was emotional piffle. It was a dodo and they would have no more of it. Instead William Wordsworth and Coleridge would write their own, ground-breaking works. A year later in 1798 the poets' *Lyrical Ballads*, which included 'The Rime of the Ancient Mariner', was published by Joseph Cottle. It was as innovative in style as it was in content. Laid out on the page with generous margins of white space, it daringly dealt with taboos such as madness and fantasy. One critic called it 'the strangest story of cock and bull that we ever saw on paper'. He would be proved wrong. *Lyrical Ballads* and the North Somerset walk which inspired it, would transform the world of poetry.

SAMUEL COLERIDGE
'I am unfortunately shoeless'

Samuel Coleridge was by no means the first of a march of poets and their admirers to undertake some furious walking in the more remote parts of Britain between 1790 and 1810. But he was the most voluble. Thomas De Quincey complained of Coleridge's 'eternal stream of talk which never for one instant intermitted, and allowed no momentary opportunity of reaction to the persecuted and fateful auditor.' Observing an admirer, John Chester, walking with Coleridge was, thought William Hazlitt, like watching 'a running footman by a state coach'.

Samuel Coleridge began serious walking in 1794 in the company of John Hucks. The two men started out from Oxford on a journey to North Wales, Hucks publishing the details of their walk in *A Pedestrian Tour through North Wales in a Series of Letters* (1795). Compared to Coleridge's sporadic letters home (the poet carried with him a black notebook and a portable ink horn so that he might, as he journeyed, 'ever and anon pluck the wild flowers of poesy, inhale their odours for a while then throw them away and think no more of them'). Hucks' account was a pedestrian report by name and by nature. He dutifully recorded the details of their 600 mile tramp as they walked to Gloucester and then Ross-on-Wye where Coleridge generously inscribed a poem on the shutter of the King's Arms. After Hereford, Leominster and Bishop's Castle, they walked on to Montgomery, Welshpool and North Wales.

Coleridge, an arch advocate of the egalitarian pantisocracy movement, a utopian society in which all members would be equal in rank and position, sought converts to the cause along the route. This lay from Welshpool to Bala, across to Llangollen, Wrexham and Ruthin, up the coast to Abergele, on to Anglesey and then down along the west coast from Caernarvon to Tregaron.

At Bala Coleridge caused a scene by declaring death to royalty in a pantisocratic toast. The high Welsh country, more populated than now, was still as bare and beautiful as it is today. As the two young men journeyed into Bala over the Berwyns the poet drank water 'as cold as ice, and clear as infant diamonds' from the wayside. At Wrexham he was disconcerted to bump into an old love from his school days, Mary Evans, while in Rhuddlan near Rhyl he was delighted by the sight of women boldly bathing naked with the local men. At Abergele he retrieved his lost walking stick from a fellow traveller with help from the town crier; and crossing the Menai Straits to Anglesey he and Hucks were almost drowned.

Hucks abandoned Coleridge, and two Cambridge friends who had joined them, during a 'fruitless and fatiguing expedition' up Snowdon. Hucks' reluctance to scale Snowdon may have been due to an earlier ascent when they climbed Penmaen Mawr during a heatwave. 'We rashly took the resolution to venture up this stupendous mountain without a guide,' wrote Hucks. Milking the episode for its full, dramatic effect, Hucks recorded that they reached the summit having surmounted 'every danger and difficulty' only to suffer 'a tormenting thirst that we were not able to gratify.' Disaster and dehydration were averted when they discovered a small, muddy spring hidden beneath a stone.

The extraordinary heat that hung over Wales that summer finally gave way to several varieties of Welsh rain when they reached Tregaron. The downpours and drizzle continued as they trudged on to Llandovery, Brecon, Abergavenny, Tintern, Chepstow and, crossing the Severn by ferry, to Bristol. Hucks concluded that, despite a lack of 'drawn beds or

William Coleridge, the poet who had difficulty maintaining a straight line as he walked. (Mary Evans Picture Library)

Turkey carpets' the walk, during which they had managed up to forty miles a day, had been excellent for 'convenience and independency'.

Five years later, Coleridge departed on a challenging three week walking tour of the Lake District, with Wordsworth and his sailor brother, John. It was his first introduction to the Cumbrian fells. Coleridge and Wordsworth had travelled up to Cumbria with their publisher Joseph Cottle who left them to walk on with John Wordsworth. Their walking tour in 1799 was to prove dramatic, demanding and satisfying for both men. Wordsworth now set his heart on returning to live in the Lakes. He would shortly relocate to Grasmere with Dorothy, and Coleridge would move to Greta Hall in Keswick a year later.

It was late autumn and the sun-burned bracken was turning nut brown as they tramped for three days from Temple Sowerby to Hawkshead (where Wordsworth had attended school), Kentmere, Troutbeck and Bowness. They stayed three days at Grasmere, 'a vision of the fair country' according to Coleridge. When John Wordsworth returned to his ship, Coleridge and Wordsworth stepped up the pace. It was by now early November and the hills towered over lakes, puckered by winter winds. It was, said Coleridge, a scene of 'simple majesty'. For the next ten days, with the weather turning cold, they walked the great routes of the Lake District, Loweswater and Crummock Water, Black Sail Pass and Wasdale Head, the dramatic Sty Head Pass and Borrowdale. They examined the Castlerigg stone circle, which they attributed to the Druids (' . . . like a dismal cirque/ Of Druid Stone', wrote John Keats in *Hyperion*) and the waterfall of Aira Force like 'a long waisted giantess slipping down on her back' wrote Coleridge. By the time the two men parted on 18 November Coleridge had turned into a seasoned fell walker.

In 1802 he returned to retrace the old routes in solitude, his knapsack filled with spare clothes, tea, sugar, pens, paper, a book of German poems and his night cap. 'I must be alone, for either my imagination or my heart are to be excited or enriched.' His lack of a companion almost deprived England of its celebrated poet when he climbed Scafell Pike and left the path to make his own, independent and highly dangerous descent to Eskdale.

Sty Head Pass in 1938, a scene of 'simple majesty' for Coleridge when he walked here in 1799. (YHA)

The next year Coleridge undertook his final, long walking tour, this time in the Scottish Highlands. And for part of the time, without his shoes. He had started out in the company of William and Dorothy, but his own melancholy had soured the general mood. Matters were not helped by his lack of laudanum. Coleridge was addicted to the infusion of opium in wine that he used to numb the pain of a mysterious illness that dogged him all his life. At Loch Lomond the three parted company, dividing up the money so that Coleridge had sufficient funds for the coach journey home from Stirling, where he proposed walking.

Free of the Wordsworths, however, Coleridge perversely strode off in the opposite direction. Over the next eight days he would walk to Fort William, on to Inverness and back to Edinburgh, an epic journey of 263 miles during which he lost his shoes. It started, Dorothy would recall in her *Recollections of a Tour Made in Scotland*, when she, William and a fellow traveller had taken the ferry-boat to Loch Katrine in the Trossachs, while the grumpy Coleridge chose to walk. 'The evening began to darken, and it rained so heavily before we had gone two miles that we were completely wet,' Dorothy wrote. 'It was dark when we landed, and on entering the house I was sick with cold.' Coleridge was in a worse state: 'I burnt my shoes in drying them at the boatman's hovel on Loch Katrine. I have by this means hurt my heel. Likewise my left leg is a little inflamed, and the rheumatism in the right of my head afflict my right eye, ear, cheek, and the three teeth.' He was still without his laudanum.

'Nevertheless', he declared after walking out on the Wordsworths, 'I am enjoying myself, having Nature with solitude and liberty.' He arrived in Edinburgh eight days later, proud of his own performance under such arduous conditions. It proved to be his last. Only thirty-one, Coleridge would undertake no more major walks.

WILLIAM WORDSWORTH
'The lonely roads were schools to me'

Coleridge could compose poetry as he walked over rough ground or broke his way through undergrowth. William Wordsworth preferred to compose as he strolled along on an even footing, for he was a walking poet. He had walked and written lines as a child in his native Cumbria: he was born at Cockermouth in 1770 and, as a schoolboy at nearby Hawkshead, regularly walked the five miles around the lake at Esthwaite before school. He enjoyed walking in the dark, running verses through his mind before committing them to paper. On one occasion he and Robert Jones, a friend from Cambridge University, climbed Snowdon from Beddgelert in the dark, just to catch sight of dawn from the summit.

> I would walk alone
> In storm and tempest, or in starlight nights
> Beneath the quiet heaven

When he and his sister Dorothy moved back to Cumbria in 1799 after living in the south, they occupied the modest Dove Cottage at Grasmere. Here Wordsworth would compose lines as he paced the gravel garden path, sheltering beneath an umbrella when it rained. By the time he reached sixty-five in 1845 the poet was said by his friend Thomas de Quincey, to have walked an estimated 180,000 miles. He had another fifteen years walking ahead of him.

In 1813, when his growing reputation, and a sinecure as Stamp Distributor, allowed him to move from Dove Cottage in Grasmere to Rydal Mount at Rydal, he continued to walk. George Venables described (and Francis Kilvert recorded) an encounter with the poet one day near Rydal when Wordsworth was 'sauntering towards me wearing a shade over his eyes, which were weak, and crooning out aloud some lines of a poem which he was composing.' Wordsworth wanted to know if the shadow of Etna would fall across Syracuse, that mountain being 40 miles from the city. 'I replied that there was nothing in the distance to prevent the shadow of the mountain falling across the city. He was evidently determined to make the shadow fall the way he wanted it. He had a perfectly independent mind and cared for no one else's opinion.'

Wordsworth had been made Poet Laureate in 1843, a civic award bestowed for his past, rather than his current, accomplishments since his powers of composition were in significant decline. Kilvert, after gossiping with Wordsworth's wife's niece, wrote in his diary of the poet's final years. 'He (Wordsworth) could not bear the act of writing and he wrote so impatiently and impetuously that his writing was rarely legible.' Yet he was walking still. 'He was very absent and has been known to walk unconsciously through a flock of sheep without perceiving them.' At seventy Wordsworth scaled Helvelyn and composed a sonnet on its summit.

William Wordsworth, the people's
poet and an indefatigable walker.
(Rydal Mount Museum)

Benjamin Robert Haydon painted a portrait of him
doing so.

Wordsworth began both serious writing and long
distance walking in 1790 when, as a Cambridge
undergraduate, he stole across the channel to
France with his friend, Robert Jones. They had
concealed their plans for a walking tour from
their tutors, fearing that they might be forbidden
to leave: three years before the guillotining of Louis
XVI, Europe was gripped by revolution fever.

There was something of Tweedle Dum and
Tweedle Dee about the pair. Jones was a rotund,
cheerful fellow and William Wordsworth tall and
gaunt. They had abandoned the conventional
woollen overcoats in favour of some curious looking, lightweight coats, and they carried their
possessions in handkerchiefs which they sometimes balanced on their heads like African village
women. But despite appearances, they were men

of mettle. Averaging up to twenty-five miles a day for over eight weeks they strode purposefully down through France, the Savoy, Switzerland and northern Italy. They rested for a boat trip on the Rhine to Cologne and then walked back to Calais. Wordsworth enjoyed himself. 'My spirits have been kept in a perpetual hurry of delight, by the almost uninterrupted succession of sublime and beautiful objects which have passed before my eyes during the course of the last month', he wrote home to Dorothy.

Wordsworth continued with a series of walking tours over the next ten years. In 1791 he and Jones took a tour through North Wales and two years later the poet made a return visit, this time on four wheels. That, at least, was the plan, but as he was travelling up from the Isle of Wight with William Calvert, Calvert's carriage was wrecked in an accident near Salisbury. Calvert took the horse and headed home. Wordsworth stepped out on to the open road and strode off along the dusty white tracks of Salisbury Plain. He walked, preoccupied by political and personal events (he was troubled by the war between France and England and worried about his affair with Annette Vallon in France which had produced a child). The route took him to Bath, Bristol, and, crossing the Severn by ferry, to Chepstow. Passing up through the Forest of Dean and the Wye valley he reached Tintern and his first glimpse of the towering remains of the Cistercian Abby, founded in 1131 and sacked in

1536. Wordsworth walked on into Wales.

Five years later, having shared pedestrial notes with Rev'd Warner in Bath, Wordsworth returned on foot to Tintern arriving in the village on July 13, 1798. He took a seat beneath a sycamore tree and gazed down on the gaunt ruins of the monastery standing beside the 'Sylvan Wye' framed by the steeply wooded, limestone cliffs.

In 'Lines composed a Few Miles from Tintern Abbey', he wrote:

> Five years have past; five summers with the length
> Of five long winters; and again I hear
> These waters, rolling from their mountain springs
> With a soft murmur. –Once again
> Do I behold these steep and lofty cliffs,
> That on a wild secluded scene impress
> Thoughts of more deep seclusion; and connect
> The landscape with the quiet of the sky.

Sometimes when a walker rests to admire the surroundings – a distant cottage on a hill, a tumble of skylarks, the lie of a ridge on the skyline – the vision will coalesce into a freeze-framed moment that, despite its apparent ordinariness, will come to mind, quite unexpectedly, months, even years later. The psychologist Abraham Maslow called them peak experiences. George Macaulay Trevelyan, a seasoned walker and one of the founders of the Youth Hostel movement, described them as 'strange, casual moments of mere sight and feeling'. They were, he wrote in *Clio, A Muse and other Essays Literary and Pedestrian* (1913) 'more vivid and less forgotten than the human events of life'. Wordsworth called them 'spots of time', transforming moments that would return, uninvited but welcome, to warm the soul and refresh the mind. His walk along the Wye and his resting place at Tintern left him with spots of time and 'imaginative impressions' which he would still recall fifty years later at Rydal Mount.

Apart from his jaunt over the Quantock Hills with Coleridge and Dorothy in 1797, Wordsworth, like Coleridge, ceased taking any more serious walking tours although he continued to walk and to advance his theories on the role of the poet. It was, he insisted, to feel and express the relationship between man and nature. Few could appreciate this so well as the seasoned walker.

In the early eighteenth century eighty per cent of the people lived and worked in the countryside. By the time he, Dorothy and Coleridge moved to Cumbria, townspeople outnumbered their rural cousins. City folk were already nostalgic for a breath of country air and the imagined country cottage with roses framing the porch. The French Revolution had frightened off those who might otherwise have trotted off on the European Grand Tour and attention turned to what the home country had to offer. With writers like Wordsworth and painters like Constable reappraising the rural scene the Victorian tourist travelled increasingly on the new steam trains, to picturesque parts of Britain, to stroll beside Ullswater, marvel at the Grampians and admire Exmoor as often as not with a copy of *Lyrical Ballads* in their gloved hands.

Byron dismissed it all as 'namy-pamby' and satirists published mocking doggerel (*'Was it a robin that I saw?/Was it a pigeon or a daw?*), but the old man who had used his power to poetise the experience familiar to anyone who walked the hills continued to charm the public.

In old age, the increasingly grumpy old man of Rydal worried about environmental matters. In particular he was concerned about landowners scarring the Cumbrian fells with their sheep walls. The hills, he said, should be protected from the ill mannered hand of man. In his *Guide to the Lakes* he considered the need to turn the Lakes into 'a sort of national property, in which every man has a right and interest who has an eye to perceive and a heart to enjoy.' After his death, his admirers seriously contemplated renaming Cumbria Wordsworthshire, but in 1951 the government of the day inaugurated a more fitting testimony to England's most famous pedestrian poet: 880 square miles of the Lake District was designated as England's largest national park, thus preserving some of Wordsworth's favourite fell walking country.

DOROTHY WORDSWORTH

'A beautiful evening, very starry, the horned moon'
Journals, March 23, 1798

While her brother and his friends wrote poetry around her, Dorothy Wordsworth did what many walkers like to do: distil their experiences into journals.

> 'The air was cold and clear – the sky blue. We walked cheerfully along in the sunshine. I never travelled with more cheerful spirits than this day.'
>
> August 20, 1803. Scotland.

She was born in Cockermouth, Cumbria a year after her brother, the third of five children. Her mother, Ann Cookson, died when Dorothy was six, and her father when she was twelve. She lived with her grandparents at Penrith and her mother's brother, William, at Forncett Rectory in Norfolk. But when her brother started to write seriously, she moved to be at his side. The relationship was close and intense. She was the 'sister of my soul', William declared and 'gave me eyes, she gave me ears.' In 1795 she helped him keep house in Dorset, then Alfoxden, and later at Dove Cottage and finally Rydal Mount. Everywhere she went, she wrote about her walks.

> 17th: 'Walked into Easedale before dinner'. 19th: 'We did not walk all day'. 20th: 'Walked to Easedale'. 21st: 'We walked all morning.' 22nd: 'In speaking of our walk on Sunday Evening . . . and the moonlight seen through

She looked frail in later years, but Dorothy Wordsworth could keep pace with both Coleridge or brother William in her youth. *(Rydal Mount Museum)*

hurrying driving clouds . . . it was a sight that I could call to mind at any time it was so distinct.' 23rd: William unwell and did not walk. 24th: 'A rainy morning. We all walked out.'

November, 1801. Grasmere.

A small, round lady in later life, the young Dorothy Wordsworth was wild eyed and dark skinned with 'a gypsy tan', according to De Quincey. And she was as good a walker as any of them. When she stayed at a friend's farm in Radnorshire or Stow Farm, Whitney in Herefordshire, the home of a Mrs Monkhouse, she thought nothing of walking from Brinsop into Hereford, six miles and back, 'if she wanted a thimble', according to Francis Kilvert. She would walk to the Hutchinson's family farm at Kington to visit her dear friend Mary (the future Mrs William Wordsworth) on the smallest excuse. On one occasion in Cumbria in 1799 Dorothy and her brother headed off for a favourite inn. The seventeen mile trip took them four hours.

> We talked of walking, but the blackness of the Cold made us slow to put forward so we did not walk at all.'
>
> January 11, 1803. Grasmere.

She was constantly at her brother's side, walking in the day, reading with him at night, listening to and copying out his poems, fretting about friends like Coleridge or lying in the grass, head to head with William, imagining as they gazed up at the clouds that they lay each in their own coffin. During her brother's most creative and consequently his busiest walking times, she became 'the beloved woman', the sister who 'in the midst of all preserved me still' (*The Preludes*). She seemed content to play the role of devotee and muse, suppressing any ambitions of her own to write, instead recording their walks and conversations in the journal which she started in the late 1790s 'to give Wm Pleasure by it.'

> We were within half a mile of Tarbet, at a sudden turning looking to the left, we saw a very craggy-topped mountain amongst other smooth ones. Framed against the lake we called out with one voice 'That's what we want!'
>
> August 20, 1803. Scotland.

During her walks she fed William with many of her ideas: in her Grasmere journal of April 15 1802, she notes a vision of daffodils in the woods close to the waterside beyond Gowbarrow Park.

> I never saw daffodils so beautiful. They grew among the mossy stones about and about them; some rested their heads upon these stones as on a pillow for weariness; and the rest tossed and reeled and danced.

In 1815 her brother published his lyrical lines:

> I wandered lonely as a cloud
> That floats on high o'er vales and hills,
> When all at once I saw a crowd,
> A host, of golden daffodils.

There was little to disrupt this close, some would say unhealthy, relationship until William married Mary Hutchinson. Dorothy could not bring herself to attend the wedding as 'I half dread that concentration of all tender feelings, past, present, and future will come to me on the wedding morning.'

For the most part, however, Dorothy's diary entries sound less like the voice of a sensitive neurotic and more like the musings of a spirited woman who loved to walk. On the final hike with Coleridge and her brother at Loch Katrine, the thirty-three-year-old Dorothy arrived at their rudimentary lodgings, cold, wet and miserable. The walkers and a fellow travel-ler ('an Edinburgh drawing-master going during the vacation on a pedestrian tour to John o' Groats' House') settle down beside the fire with a dram of whisky, sugar, butter and barley-bread. Dorothy described how the house was divided into three with the cow house at one end, a combined dairy and bedroom at the other and the kitchen and the house fire in the centre. The rooms were partitioned only up to the eaves so that the kitchen fire flickered across the ceilings of all three. The beams, she wrote, were varnished black with fire smoke and glistened 'glossy as black rocks on a sunny day caught in ice'.

> We caroused in our cups of coffee, laughing like children at the strange atmosphere in which we were. The smoke came in gusts, and spread along the walls and above our heads in the chimney, where the hens were roosting like clouds in the sky. I had never felt so deeply the blessing of a hospitable welcome and a warm fire.'

Her description is reminiscent of many a cosy winter's night spent in some remote backpackers' lodge. As she lay on her clean, dry bed of chaff, (Coleridge, her brother and the other traveller bedded down in the barns), she watches the firelight flickering on the beams and listens to the rain beating down on the lake outside. The host family leave the kitchen and creep into their bed at the far side of her room. 'I did not sleep much, but passed a comfortable night . . . the unusualness of my situation prevented me from sleeping. I could hear the waves beat against the shore of the lake. When I sat up in bed I could see the lake through an open window-place at the bed's head.'

The long walk, the whisky, the warm bed and the

rain on the lake combine to make a memorable moment for Dorothy, what William might have called another spot of time. The following day the woman of the house tells Dorothy repeatedly that she will remember the night for the rest of her life. Sadly Dorothy, who often complains of headaches in her diary, would soon forget everything.

Old James was the loyal gardener at Rydal Mount where Dorothy died in 1855, five years after her brother. James was not above gossiping about its famous residents and he revealed to one William Howitt (who repeated it to Miss Hutchinson from the Rectory at Whitney who, in her turn, repeated it to Francis Kilvert) that Dorothy had suffered physically and mentally as she grew older. It was said that, having been a great walker in her youth, she had over taxed herself. Dorothy, he revealed, had lapsed into apparent imbecility, hiding from visitors and playing obsessively with bowls of soapsuds. Although she had occasional lucid moments she soon slipped back into a vegetative state. The cause of her demise was blamed on over walking. George Venables told Kilvert of a meeting with William and Dorothy shortly before the poet's death. 'Dorothy was in the room, an old woman by this time. Her brother told me he attributed the failure of her health and intellect to the long walks she used to take with him.' In reality Dorothy's shared passion for pedestrianism probably did her more good than harm. She was almost certainly suffering from the effects of a thiamin deficiency brought on by arterio-sclerosis.

WILLIAM HAZLITT
'Give me the clear blue sky over my head'

> 'Give me the clear blue sky over my head, and the green
> turf beneath my feet, a winding road before me, and a
> three hours' march to dinner – and then to thinking. I
> laugh, I run, I leap, I sing for joy.'

If there is an anthem to walking it is here in the words
of the essayist and philosopher William Hazlitt. He
wrote his essay *On Going a Journey* in *Table Talk* 1822,
the first to be devoted entirely to the pleasures of
pedestrianism and one which Robert Louis Stevenson
carried (together with a copy of *Tristram Shandy*) on
his own walking excursions. 'One of the pleasantest
things in the world is going on a journey,' continued
Hazlitt. 'But I like to go by myself . . . I cannot see
the wit of walking and talking at the same time. I
like solitude.'

The son of a Unitarian minister, also called
William, of Wem in Shropshire, William Hazlitt had
abandoned his own studies to become a minister
and decided to become a man of letters instead.
By the time he penned his hymn to hiking he had
already journeyed in the company of one of the
great walkers of his age, Samuel Coleridge. He met
Coleridge when the poet travelled up from Somerset
to preach at Shrewsbury and to consider taking
up the post of preacher. The young Hazlitt deeply
admired Coleridge (although he would eventually

fall out with both Coleridge and Wordsworth) and to reach the church in time Hazlitt had to leave before dawn. On foot. 'Never, the longest day I have to live, shall I have such another walk as this cold, raw, comfortless one in the winter of the year 1798,' he would recall later. But Coleridge did not disappoint: 'Poetry and Philosophy had met together,' declared Hazlitt. 'This was even beyond my hopes.' Returning the ten miles to Wem, Hazlitt was in ecstasy. He saw in the pale, winter's sun and 'the cold dank drops of dew that hung half melted on the beard of the thistle . . . a spirit of hope and youth in all nature, that turned every thing into good'.

After his sermon at Shrewsbury, Coleridge came to stay at the Hazlitt household in Wem to wrestle over the decision about whether or not to become a paid preacher. He was relieved to learn, as he arrived at the Hazlitt household, that the decision had been made for him. The wealthy Wedgwood family, which owned the booming china manufacturing business, had decided to settle on him an endowment of £150 so that he might devote his energies to poetry rather than the religious niceties of Unitarianism. The delighted Coleridge decided to leave Wem immediately and return to Nether Stowey with the news. Rather than take the coach from Wem to Shrewsbury, Coleridge decided to walk through the January frosts. The crestfallen Hazlitt volunteered to walk by his side for part of the journey. While he noted for the first time Coleridge's annoying habit of continually stepping into his companion's path, Hazlitt was dazzled by

1798 and winter walking was 'cold, raw and comfortless'.

the poet's conversation. Coleridge took to the young man and invited him to come and stay with him later in the year.

Anticipating the strenuous walks that lay ahead, Hazlitt determined to prepare himself mentally and physically for his visit to Nether Stowey with a walk to Llangollen, about twenty miles distant. Compared with his freezing walk to Shrewsbury in January, his journey to Llangollen was an April delight. He walked up the Dee valley, which 'opened like an amphitheatre, broad, barren hills rising in majestic state on either side', on the day of his twentieth birthday. Lines of Coleridge's, which he had just learned, about valleys that 'glittered green with sunny showers' and the 'green upland swells that echo to the bleat of flocks' were brought to life in the surrounding landscape. It was a contented and inspired twenty year old who on 10 April, 1798 sat down at an inn in Llangollen and devoured a bottle of sherry and a cold chicken as he read his copy of *New Eloise* by Jean-Jacques Rousseau. Having digested all three he felt ready to

'Give me the clear blue sky over my head.' Hazlitt wrote an anthem to the joys of walking. (Mary Evans Picture Library)

walk on 'along the high road that overlooks the delicious prospect, repeating the lines which I have just quoted from Mr Coleridge's poems'.

Thus prepared Hazlitt left for Nether Stowey on foot. He walked by way of Shrewsbury, Worcester, and Tewkesbury (where he was soaked in a downpour), Gloucester, Bristol and finally Bridgwater, near Nether Stowey. In his youthful enthusiasm he had covered the 150 miles so fast that he was two days early. He had to wait in Bridgwater, keeping boredom at bay by reading Frances Burney's latest novel, *Camilla*, until Coleridge was ready to receive him. He then spent the next three weeks walking and listening to Coleridge and that other inspiring walker,

Wordsworth.

One day they walked from Nether Stowey to Alfoxden, Wordsworth reading and performing as he did so. Towards the end of his stay Hazlitt walked the Somerset and Devon coast to Lynton with Coleridge and one of the poet's great devotees, John Chester. Chester not only accompanied Coleridge 'like a running footman', but was attracted to him, wrote Hazlitt, 'as flies are to honey': always the honest intellectual, Hazlitt did not enjoy such scenes of sycophancy. The three men, led by Coleridge, retraced much of the famous walk which the poet had taken with Dorothy and William Wordsworth the year before. On the first of the three day journey they walked almost forty miles, through the little sandy resort of Blue Anchor and picturesque Dunster, which, with its old watermill, dovecot and market house, reminded Hazlitt of a scene from a painting by Poussin. They were still some distance from Lynton, the sun low in the west, when from the top of a summit, probably Selworthy Beacon which rises here to 308m, Hazlitt pointed out to his companions a ship at rest in Bridgwater Bay. Its rigging framed by the blood-red setting sun reminded Hazlitt of Coleridge's stricken ship in 'The Rime of the Ancient Mariner'.

They reached the inn at Lynton, almost certainly the same one as Coleridge had stayed at the previous year. The shutters were down and the lights all out, but they knocked the landlord up and put up here for the next two nights, Hazlitt being particularly taken by the rambler's breakfast they received, 'tea, toast,

Hazlitt's delicious prospect: Llangollen and the Dee Valley. (Arkitype)

eggs, and honey, in the very sight of the bee hives from which it had been taken, and a garden full of thyme and wild flowers that had produced it.' The next day three men strolled up the famous Valley of Rocks, a scene which Coleridge and Wordsworth once planned as the setting for a novel based on the biblical murder story of Cain and Abel. Later they walked on the beach and heard from the local fisherman the sad story of a boy who had drowned the previous day and of their efforts to rescue him.

The following day they walked back to Nether Stowey and Hazlitt turned for home, once again on foot. Although it was thirty-three miles from Bridgwater, Coleridge obligingly accompanied him as far as Bristol.

Having acquired a taste for tramping from Coleridge, Hazlitt continued to walk regularly. In 1822 he seems to have taken to the trail to recover from an unfortunate love affair. He had been crossed in love by Sarah Walker, the daughter of a couple who ran a London lodging house in which he had stayed, and for whom he had divorced his wife. Hazlitt undertook a walking tour of Loch Lomond and the Trossachs from Glasgow with Sheridan Knowles, the owner of the Glasgow Free Press. 'It is because I want a little breathing-space to muse on indifferent matters that I absent myself from town for a while', he wrote of the affair. But he was too distraught to enjoy the walk. Unable to climb Ben Lomond 'clad in air and sunshine' . . . and snow, he abandoned the walk. A year later he was walking with a friend, Peter Patmore, under the 'broiling sunshine' in Hampshire to view some portraits by Sir Richard Colt Hoare. Patmore noted 'the extraordinary physical as well as moral effect produced on Hazlitt by the sight and feel of the country. His look (was) eager and onward, as if devouring the way before it – his whole air buoyant and triumphant.'

His experiences of walking with Coleridge, with Patmore, and above all alone, led Hazlitt to reflect on the benefits of taking a hike instead of a carriage. 'We go a journey chiefly to be free of all impediments and of all inconvenience; to leave ourselves behind.'

THOMAS DE QUINCEY
'Happier life I cannot image than this vagrancy'

Thomas De Quincey was another walking man who found himself entangled in the Wordsworths' lives. De Quincey became a household name when, in 1822, he published the *Confessions of an English Opium Eater*, a wild and creative account of thirty years addiction to the drug (which, at the time, was commonly used by politicians, preachers and nursing mothers alike).

He was received by Wordsworth in 1807 – he was an ardent fan of the *Lyrical Ballads* – and became a close family friend, renting Dove Cottage at Grasmere when William and Dorothy moved to Rydal Mount. (The close relationship might have continued – there was talk of his marrying Dorothy – but De Quincey instead married a local farmer's daughter, Margaret Simpson, after having a child with her, in 1817.) It was De Quincey who observed in his *Literary Reminiscences* (1839) that Wordsworth's famous legs, reputed to have carried the poet for over 175,000 miles, had nevertheless been condemned by every woman he knew. Yet, he conceded, they worked well enough in 'a mode of exertion which . . . stood in the stead of alcohol and all other stimulants'. De Quincey knew about such things: like Coleridge, his head was already muddled with opium.

He had started taking the drug as a student at Oxford, and now, while he continued taking it, offset its effects by walking. '(I) am never thoroughly in health unless when having pedestrian exercise to the extent of fifteen miles at the most, eight to ten miles at the least.' He walked off the opiates with the faith of the neurotic, hatless and in all weathers.

De Quincey shared Wordsworth's strange fondness for walking in the dark. Anyone who has walked home from a country pub on a moonless, cloudy night knows the apprehension of following one's hands down the road, praying they encounter nothing. It did not worry De Quincey. 'I took the greatest delight in these nocturnal walks through the silent valleys of Cumberland and Westmoreland.'

Where did this obsessive behaviour originate? It was not from the Wordsworths. De Quincey's first long walk was through the school gates of the prestigious Manchester Grammar School. By the age of 16, in 1802, De Quincey had tired of his tutorials. He wrote to a lady family friend begging for five guineas – she sent ten – and, with two more he had saved, he stole out of school 'on foot – carrying a small parcel, with some articles of dress, under one arm, a favourite English poet in one pocket; and a small volume containing about nine plays of Euripides, in the other.'

He walked the thirty-eight miles to Chester where he persuaded his reluctant mother (she was recently widowed; the return of her dying husband to the family home one darkening evening was a memory which haunted De Quincey all his life) that a long walk would do him good. Then, convincing an obliging uncle to settle an allowance of a guinea a week on him, he embarked on a series of gentle, walking

Thomas De Quincey was a passionate walker, despite his opiate addiction. (Mary Evans Picture Library)

adventures in Wales.

For a while he lodged in a family home. When the landlady was warned by her former employer, a bishop, about the risks of letting rooms to swindlers, she mentioned her concerns to him. The headstrong De Quincey strode out of the house, considering briefly mailing a letter in Greek to the meddling bishop complaining about his interference.

For a while he stays in taverns. 'A world-wearied man . . . could not do better than revolve amongst these modest inns in the five northern Welsh counties of Denbigh, Montgomery, Carnarvon, Merioneth, and Cardigan.' He was now walking from Shrewsbury through Llangollen to Llanwrst ('an alarming word to the eye' but easily pronounced 'Llanroost') Conway, Bangor, through Caernarfon and Dolgellau, Harlech,

Barmouth and 'through the sweet solitudes of Cardiganshire.'

The first few nights De Quincey spent with 'fellow-tourists in the quiet little cottage parlours of the Welsh posting houses' where the local harpist could be relied on for a song or two. He shared journey tales with other travellers whom he called 'fugitive members of our society'. They included a couple of Welsh lawyers who touted their business around the market towns and who tell him: 'Wales, as is pretty well known breeds a population somewhat litigious'. A young German, De Haren, gave him language lessons (although not in Welsh) and directed De Quincey to an inn south of Dolgellau where the mistress of the house worked as cook, waiter, chambermaid, boots and ostler and charged only six pence for a night's rest. De Quincey returned to the inn thirteen years later on a walk from Cardiff to Bangor and found this excellent hostess still slaving away, this time polishing a pair of boots before preparing 'the elegant office of greasing a horse's heels.' That night a dance is held at the inn at which the landlady 'had, I dare say, to ply the fiddle.' The noise of dancing finally gives way at three in the morning to what De Quincey called the sweetest female voice singing in the parlour below. 'She was a stranger; a visitor from some distance; and (I was told in the morning) a Methodist.'

Back on his first walk, De Quincey had run into financial difficulties and was forced to make economies. Seventeenth century Wales was as inexpensive

and accommodating as twentieth century Cambodia and, apart from one frugal period when he was forced to live on blackberries, hips and haws, he had difficulty spending more than three shillings a week on a walking diet of milk, goat's meat, potatoes and fresh water fish including best quality trout. 'Tea or coffee there was none: and I did not at that period very much care for either.'

The cost of accommodation, however, was mounting up. Since the price of a daily servant and a nightly bed ran to half a guinea a day he took to sleeping out. His policy was 'if the autumnal air was warm enough, to save the expense of a bed and the chambermaid by sleeping amongst the ferns and furze upon a hillside.' He considered carrying a heavy cloak or 'an Arab's burnoose' but rejected it on the grounds of weight. Instead he constructed what must have been one of the first one-man tents, an ingenious canvass shelter 'not larger than an ordinary umbrella.' Sleeping out of doors brings about natural anxieties as dark descends and De Quincey, comforted by the absence of Welsh jaguars, pumas or anacondas, nevertheless confessed to an irrational fear that some 'Brahminical-looking cow' will step on his face in the night.

When he was not sleeping amongst dangerous cows, he carried out some letter writing in exchange for the occasional night's accommodation. One such spell of casual hospitality included a stay with four sisters who let him in while their parents were away at a Methodist conference in Caernarfon. In return for writing the sisters' love letters he is given a bed which he shares with their three brothers. When, inevitably, the parents return, De Quincey attempts to ingratiate himself with them. Stone-faced they tell him: 'Dym sassenach' (no English) and he leaves in a hurry. On the road again, and on the last leg of his journey, he reflects on the bitter fruits of old age. 'Unless powerfully counteracted by all sorts of opposite agencies, it is a miserable corrupter and blighter to the genial charities of the human heart.'

By the age of seventy he could grumble with the best of them. He recalled the construction of a mail-coach road in Grasmere as being carried out by vandals, defrauding the parish and an outrage to the

vale. But he was also still walking. 'Breakfast time
. . . is always a cheerful stage of the day; if a man
can forget his cares at any season, it is then; and
(after) a walk of seven miles it is doubly so.'

EDWARD THOMAS
'Much has been written of travel, far less of the road'

It's 1912 and a blazing hot summer's day has been
interrupted by a shower of rain in the Berkshire
village of Blewbury. The tall, slim, blue-eyed young
man who had swung along the village street with
a long slow stride, steps under the overhang of a
barn roof to shelter. He carries a staff cut from a
hedgerow sapling and is dressed in a dusty Burberry
and baggy trousers. He lacks a hat and his fine,
fair hair is bleached by the sun. Impatient to be
moving again, he steps out on the road and walks
away in the rain.

'According to custom I stood under the broad,
overhanging eaves of Blewbury's thatched roof
and watched the rain, but it was better to be in
it and to smell the wetted dust. I was glad to feel,
to hear, to smell and to taste, and to see the rain
falling.'

The author was the poet Edward Thomas, walking from Thetford in Norfolk to Wanborough in
Wiltshire in order to explore the ancient Icknield
Way and to write a book about it. 'A great many
must be walking over England nowadays with the
primary object of writing books,' he wrote, himself

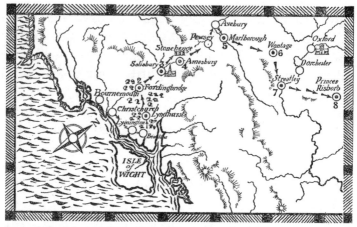

Part of the Icknield Way, 'full of the sense of roads', wrote Thomas.

the author of over thirty. 'It has not been decided whether this is a worthy object,' added Thomas who had a particular dislike of rural hacks and the sentimental ramblings of what he called 'bungalow countrymen'.

The Icknield Way was published four years later, after Thomas had enlisted with the Artists' Rifles for service in the First World War. His book detailed his ten day journey through Thetford, Newmarket, Royston, Letchworth, Streatley, Wendover, Chinnor, Wallingford, Wantage and Wanborough, outside Swindon. He recorded little details on the way, such as an old woman near Royston, 'thin, hawkfaced, bare and brown to the breast, with glittering blue eyes, and in her upper jaw, three strong teeth'. She tells him: '"You are thin, boy."' On his third night, in Edlesborough he falls asleep in a clean and comfortable bed 'while stone-curlews were piping on the downs and a pair of

126

country wheels were rolling by, late and slow.' On the fifth day, walking from Ivinghoe to Watlington 'we see no man, nor smoke, and hear no noises of man or beast or machinery, and straightway one recalls very early mornings when London has lain silent but for the cooing of pigeons.' The naturalist in him observes butterflies chasing one another, 'sometimes a white after a brown', the sun being 'perfect for them' as he makes his way from Streatley to Sparsholt. Walking the Ridgeway and looking down from Whitehorse Hill on the English countryside before the morning mists have burned away, he sees the landscape as a chain of islands – the Downs, the Chilterns, Gog Magog, the Mendips, the Cotswolds and Quantocks – linked by the thread of his track.

His cross country passage sounds out a litany of English village names: Lackford, Kentford, Ickleton (which took its name from the Way), Odsey, Whiteleaf, Ipsden and Cleeve, Aston Clinton, Weston Turville, Ewelme, Blewbury, East Hendred, Ashbury and Bishopstone. He strode through each, wondering why he should have to walk and, once, wishing to be rescued by any form of transport, except a pair of hob-nailed boots.

Yet walking was 'of all his pleasures . . . the deepest and the most comprehensive', according to his wife, Helen, writing in a later edition of *The South Country* (1909). He walked, she wrote, for all sorts of reasons, for exercise, as a lover of nature, 'as the aesthete satisfying his eye with the beauty of the contours of the hills', as the wayfarer and as the artist 'transmut-

Walking for Edward Thomas was the 'deepest and most comprehensive' of his pleasures. (Mary Evans Picture Library)

ing all this into words.' He walked also as a way of dealing with depression.

Thomas was a working walker: 'I walk because it is necessary to do so in order both to live and to make a living'. And *The Icknield Way* was a book less about his journey than about the road 'which begins many miles before I could come on its traces and ends many miles beyond where I had to stop.'

The present 105 mile Icknield Way Path, from Knettishall Heath in Norfolk to Ivinghoe Beacon in Buckinghamshire, lies along one of the old roads of Britain. Parts of the path lie buried beneath the traffic which bundles along the A11 between Norwich and London, although much of Thomas' 1913 route still follows the same farm tracks and footpaths today.

The Icknield Way was a trade route, and stone axes unearthed along its route suggest it had been

Thomas willed the Icknield Way towards the tomb of Giraldus at St David's. (Arkitype)

walked since Neolithic times. Thomas believed it had been as important to religious communities as it had been to the Stone Age axe traders and that it would have crossed the country from the east, leading the evangelising Christians from the East Anglian Wash to somewhere such as St Michael's Mount in Cornwall, or 'by the Ceidrych Valley, along the Towy to Caermarthen' and St David's in Pembrokeshire, 'now as holy as Rome.' (He willed the route towards Wales: 'the utmost reward for this conjecturing traveller would be to find himself on the banks of the Towy or, beside the tomb of Giraldus at St David's itself.')

Walkers such as Coleridge, Wordsworth, Hazlitt and De Qunicey had walked to record their pedestrian impressions: Thomas was interested in the road itself. The road, he argued, was a rich subject for contemplation and, while there were a thousand good reasons to take a walk, there was no better reason than to study the road itself. He repeats the wag's reply to the question 'Where does this road go?' ('I've lived here sixteen years and it's not moved yet.') But, wrote Thomas, roads do move. 'Some roads creep, some continue merely; some advance with majesty, some mount a hill in curves like a soaring seagull.'

Thomas returned to write his book at the family home in Steep, Petersfield near Bedales school where his wife Helen taught. Thomas was already a well-respected literary journalist whose circle of friends included Walter de la Mare, Hector Hugh Munro (the short story writer Saki) and another walker, W.H. Davies ('What is this life if, full of care, We have no time to stand and stare?'). The American poet Robert Frost would shortly to be added to the list.

From 1911 to 1913 a groups of poets including Frost and Thomas gravitated towards the apple orchard covered countryside around Dymock, where Gloucestershire borders on Herefordshire. The future poet laureate, John Masefield, was already there and Frost, who had been frustrated by his failure to break into the literary scene back home in America, moved to live at Little Iddens, a labourer's cottage at Leadington with his wife and four children. He noted that the local meadows were covered with yellow daffodils, the wild 'lent lilies' gathered by the locals and sent for sale on the grimy streets of Birmingham and Merthyr.

Eleanor Farjeon (she wrote the hymn 'Morning has Broken') rented Glyn Iddens and Wilfred Wilson Gibson, already an established poet, moved to The Old Nail Shop. Thomas and Frost regularly criss-crossed the field paths to visit him and spend time under the black timbers and rosy brick of the old house. Then in 1913 the seal of fame was set on the Dymock group with the arrival of Rupert Brooke, the tragic high priest of the pre-war poets. Brooke's 'The Soldier' ('If I should die, think only this of me: that there's some corner of a foreign field that is forever England') was published in the final issue of their periodical, *New Numbers*, which was distributed by the group.

In his poem 'The Golden Room', Gibson recalled a summer evening at the Old Nailshop:

Our neighbours from The Gallows, Catherine
And Lascelles Abercrombie; Rupert Brooke;
Elinor and Robert Frost, living awhile
At Little Iddens, who'd brought over with them
Helen and Edward Thomas. In the lamplight
We talked and laughed

The talk had been serious stuff, not unlike the conversations between Coleridge and Wordsworth concerning the creation of a new and honest poetry. And like Coleridge and Wordsworth much of the serious talk took place as Abercrombie, Frost, Brooke and Thomas tramped the surrounding countryside. These were not long distance walks, but, like Kilvert's 'villaging

The Old Nail Shop where Thomas and the walking Dymock poets often gathered. (Arkitype)

about', short strolls through summery green lanes, alongside the river Leadon, more stream than river, or up and over the rounded bulk of May Hill where the view from its summit, nippled with a plantation of Scots firs, reputedly looked out on ten counties.

Thomas' time with Frost persuaded the author to spend more writing time on his poetry. He was on a journey to rejoin the poets in the summer of 1914 when he penned his famous lines: 'Yes. I remember Aldestrop/when the Gloucester train pulled up in the village'. By the end of the year Thomas, after rejecting Frost's invitation to return with him to America, joined the Artists' Rifles. He was killed by a German shell on Easter Monday, 1917, during the battle of Arras.

In his introduction to *The Icknield Way* which he dedicated to his friend and fellow walker, Henry Hooton, he had written: 'The end is in the means – in the sight of that beautiful line of the Downs in which a curve is latent – in the houses we shall never enter, with their dark secret windows and quiet hearth smoke or the ruins friendly only to elders and nettles – in the people passing which we shall never know though we may love them.'

Footnote: The rucksack

A bulging rucksack, wrote the Ramblers Association's Tom Stephenson, speaks of inexperience rather than a stout heart. So what to pack? And what to leave out?

John Hillaby in his book *Walking Through Britain* recorded how he was in the habit of conducting a roll call of the contents of his rucksack every morning before he set off: John Feltham offered advice on what those items should be. The walker should 'have about him all his real necessaries; these are but few, a single change of linen, a pocket map, compass, &c. which take but little space.' Pastor Moritz in 1782 was satisfied with 'four guineas, some linen, and my English book of the roads, and a map and pocket-book, together with Milton's *Paradise Lost*.' Meanwhile, John Taylor, to 'pay hunger's fees', carried 'good bacon, biscuit, neat's tongue, cheese with roses, barberries, of each conserves, and mithridate, that vigorous health preserves.'

Taylor used the word rucksack: Feltham went into more detail. 'A small neat bag made with oil-case and lined, about 15 inches every way, made to button deep

to prevent rain penetrating, and four buttons to fasten two shoulder-belts, will form a knapsack of small weight and attended with no inconvenience.' He advised the backpacker to ignore the 'false shame which may arise from its pedlar-like appearance'. However he conceded that in order to secure a polite reception and a better bed when reaching town the pack could be concealed in a copious 'handkerchief . . . large enough for two persons.' Like George Borrow, Feltham also believed that 'a light small umbrella was a 'desirable addition.'

John Hucks, Coleridge's walking companion, in his *Tour through Wales* (1794) denounced those who discriminated against the walker and his 'wallet or knapsack'. All right, he agreed: the rucksack might be neither fashionable nor gentlemanly, but if he were to encounter an acquaintance 'who would be ashamed of me and my knapsack . . . I should . . . be induced to pity and to despise him for his weakness'.

In some circumstances, however, discretion was clearly the better part of valour. When Robert Louis Stevenson was arrested by suspicious police at Châtillon-sur-Loire while walking with his friend Walter Simpson he was obliged to turn out the contents of his rucksack before a local magistrate to satisfy the dignitary that he was not a dealer in pornography. The contents included two volumes of poetry, a map, a change of shirts, of shoes, of socks, and of linen trousers, a small dressing-case and a piece of soap in one of the shoes. He was promptly locked up.

CHAPTER 4

BRINGING IT TO BOOK

JOHN TAYLOR
Six hundred miles, I (very neere) have footed

In the opening decades of the seventeenth century as Cervantes was publishing his *Adventures of Don Quixote*, a Gloucestershire man was committing his own adventures to paper. Despite having suffered the indignity of having one of his earlier works burned in public, John Taylor was about to publish the first account of a walking tour through Britain.

The *Penniless Pilgrimage* (1618) detailed his journey on foot from London to Edinburgh, in the same year as Ben Jonson. Taylor knew of Jonson's plans to publish his own walker's account and could not

136

hope to rival Jonson's literary reputation. Taylor, however, had a gimmick: he would, he promised, travel light, so light that he would be 'not carrying any Money to and fro, neither Begging, Borrowing, or Asking Meate, drinke or Lodging'.

Hardships were inevitable: overtaken by nightfall on the lonely Dunsmoor Heath north of Daventry, he was forced to bivouac in a field under a make-shift shelter of ferns and rushes, sharing his open air lodgings with four cows, two steers and a bull. Nevertheless Taylor is entranced by the nightscape:

In heaven's star-chamber I did lodge that night;
Ten thousand stars me to my bed did light.

The weather was less kind some days later when he was again forced to sleep in a field just beyond the small Trent valley town of Stone in Staffordshire. To keep away the rain, which fell steadily for six hours, he erected a 'pavilion' of broom and hay.

Although the highways were busy with traders and tramps, Taylor was the object of constant curiosity. He complained of being treated as if he was 'some monster sent from Mogul' or 'some strange beast from the Amazonian queen', but managed to maintain a sense of humour: reaching Blythe in Nottinghamshire 'so near dead' with exhaustion he is 'blythe . . . to come to any place of harbour'. Still travelling penniless he spends one night in a house where he is 'enforced to rise, I was so stung with Irish musquitoes, a creature that . . . do inhabit and breed most in sluttish houses'. And this house, he adds, 'was none of the cleanest'. Taylor reached Edinburgh, but evidently decided the capital was too modest a goal. He pressed on for Aberdeen. Passing over the Grampian foothills, his teeth chattering with the cold, he crossed 'craggy hills and thunder-battered chills' so precipitous that 'a dog with three legs would outrun a horse with four.'

On the face of it this is a remarkable account of a remarkable walk by a remarkable man. (Taylor was also lame in one leg after being injured as a young man when he was press ganged into the navy). That, however, is the face of it. The reality was rather different.

John Taylor funded his journey by raising his own advance on the promised book (the average seventeenth century book publisher did not pay an advance on book sales) and for *Penniless Pilgrimage* the walking author sold what he called his Taylor's Bills to around 1,600 customers before publication.

After publication of *Penniless Pilgrimage or The Moneylesse perambulation, of John Taylor, Alias the King's Majestie's Water-poet*, over half his subscribers refused to pay up. For the book revealed that, while Taylor had walked, he had the company of a servant and a pack horse. The horse's saddle bags contained enough food for a small banquet. He had also been feted and fed by friends (including, as we have seen, Ben Jonson in Edinburgh) and the business of crossing those 'craggy hills' had been undertaken in the company of the Earl of Mar during a monumental deer hunt.

John Taylor, author,
if not true advocate,
of the 1618 *Penniless
Pilgrimage* (The Company
of Watermen and
Lightermen of the River
Thames)

John Taylor had been born in Gloucester on 24 August 1580. His impoverished parents scraped together the funds to send him to the grammar school for an education which must have prepared him for a literary life. Leaving school, however, he was apprenticed to a Thames waterman. His fresh-water ferrying led to life on the open waves: he was nabbed by one of the press gangs who preyed on young men and pressed into service with good Queen Bess' navy. An ardent Royalist, Taylor duly served his monarch for sixteen voyages before retiring with his leg injury. He returned to the river bank, but trade was tight and the sailor turned author. For the next forty years the Water Poet, or literary bargee as he was sometimes known, travelled and wrote about his travels.

He supplemented his income with inn keeping,

running a tavern at Oxford and later the Crown in Phoenix Alley, Longacre where he wore his Royalist sympathies on his inn sign. When, in 1649, King Charles I was beheaded by Oliver Cromwell's Parliamentary supporters, Taylor renamed the Crown the Mourning Crown. Threatened with reprisals by Parliamentary supporters he changed the name to the Poet's Head and had his own portrait painted on the inn sign.

Taylor was a showman and some of his early journeys, including several by ship, were publicity-seeking stunts. One, which has all the hallmarks of having been conceived after a late night in the bar, involved he and a vintner rowing down the Thames from London to Queensborough in Kent in a boat made of brown paper and powered by oars fashioned from two canes and a pair of dead fish. The travel writer was almost drowned when the boat foundered. His survival served only to heighten the profile of this publicity-conscious author.

Prior to the *Penniless Pilgrimage*, Taylor poked a little fun at Thomas Coryate in *Laugh and Be Fat*, published in 1913. Coryate, naturally offended, persuaded a few friends to publicly burn Taylor's tome. When in 1617 Taylor travelled from London to Hamburg (although not on foot) he dedicated his *Three Weekes, three daies, and three houres Observation and Travel, from London to Hamburgh in Germanie* to 'Sir Tho. Coryate. Knight of Troy, and of the dearest darlings to the Blind Goddess Fortune'.

Taylor lived up to Horace Walpole's assertion that 'when men write for profit they are not very delicate'. As 'a youth of threescore and ten' he travelled from London to Land's End. 'Six hundred miles, I (very neere) have footed' he wrote in *Wanderings to see the Wonders of the West*, adding that he was neither 'sho'd nor booted' for the entire journey. Once again testimony and truth were ill-matched: and once again he gave the game away in his account. He confessed to wearing 'light buskins', to begging lifts and frequently hiring a horse. After another 600 mile tour through Wales and, in 1653, a shorter journey through Kent and Sussex, John Taylor the Water Poet died and was buried, in truth, at London's St Martin-in-the-Fields.

WILLIAM HUTTON
'Every man has his hobby horse: I ride mine on foot'

One fine day in 1795 a Birmingham businessman, William Hutton, set out to view a property that he thought he might buy in the quiet Worcestershire town of Tenbury Wells. The distance from the city of Birmingham to Tenbury was thirty eight miles. In spite of his age – Hutton was seventy-two – and being well able afford a carriage and horses, he chose Shank's Pony instead. 'Providence has favoured me with limbs. It was but gratitude to use them,' he explained.

During his journey through the bosky byways of the Midlands William Hutton reflected upon his life. It was a trick of his designed to pass the time pleasantly. He had trained himself to 'recollect an anecdote, as insignificant and remote as I was able' for every year of his life 'rejecting all under ten years old.' (When he detailed them in a little book he found he was missing only nine days of his life) In fact his memory of life as an eight year old was sharp enough as he later recalled in his memoirs, *The Life of William Hutton* (1815).

Born in Derby in 1723 he had been apprenticed to a local sweatshop where he started work at five every morning. He recalled the terror of waking in the night and, seeing light on the ceiling, being convinced that he was late for the loom. 'I rose in tears, for fear of punishment, and went to my father's bedside, to ask the time. He believed six: I darted out in agonies. Observing no lights in the mill, I knew it was

A commemorative plaque to William
Hutton, historian and walker, in Derby.
(Derby City Council)

an early hour, the reflection of snow had deceived
me. Returning, the town clock struck two.'

Life at the silk mill deprived Hutton of his childhood. 'There were three hundred persons employed
there, I was the youngest. I had to submit to the cane
whenever convenient to the master; (and) be the
constant companion of the most rude and vulgar
of the human race'. His father marked the boy's
tenth birthday by presenting him not with a hoop
or a spinning top, but a 'quart of twopenny beer'
to commemorate the occasion. There was little to
celebrate: in the same year his mother died giving
birth to his eighth sibling while his father tried to
drown his sorrows in drink. Curiously when Hutton
lost his own wife Sarah years later Hutton took, not
to the bottle, but to walking.

Hutton left the mill at fourteen and was apprenticed by an uncle to more hard labour, this time as a
silk stockinger in Nottingham. When his uncle died
the now twenty-six year old seized the opportunity
to start his own business and opened a book binding

shop in Southwell. There was one problem: the shop lay fourteen miles from his home in Nottingham. But Hutton evidently thought nothing of making a daily, twenty-eight mile round trip to and from the shop on foot. He was more vexed by the people of Southwell who were proud enough of their fruit stocks (the town was reputed to be the birthplace of the Bramley apple), but less enthusiastic about literary matters. In 1750 Hutton was forced to shut the shop and open one in Birmingham instead.

Gradually his fortunes began to improve. He started Birmingham's first paper warehouse, nearly bankrupted the family investing in a paper mill, and then successfully speculated on property. He built a country house at Bennett's Hill, wrote a *History of Birmingham* in 1782 and was elected to the Antiquarian Society of Scotland in the same year. Aside from some unpleasant business over his religious convictions (rioters fired both of the Quaker's homes in 1791 despite or perhaps because of his buying the demonstrators 329 gallons of ale) he was now earning good money and spending a good proportion of it on travel.

But for now, as he walked on to Tenbury between cart tracks and listened to the cuckoo in the woods and the swallows above, he fretted about the health of his own 'dear love', his wife Sarah whom he had married in 1755 and who had borne him a family before her recent illness. He and his daughter Catherine devoted much of their time to her care and he worried about taking time away from her bedside.

As Tenbury's twelfth-century church spire hove in sight, he comforted himself with the knowledge that he would be back with Sarah by the following day. At seventy-two Hutton still regarded a walk of seventy-six miles in a day as perfectly manageable.

The following year his dear Sarah died and Mr Hutton, a man who 'owed much to Nature, and nothing to Education', according to a friend, resumed his walks. Dressed in black, an apparel he described as 'a kind of religious travelling warrant', he carried his maps, notebook, pen and ink bottle in a black 'budget . . . much like a dragoon's cartridge box, or post-man's letter pouch. To this little packet I fastened with a string, an umbrella in a green case,' hanging it over 'that shoulder which was least tired.' His daughter described her father's gait as 'like a saunter', a pace at which the stocky gentleman managed

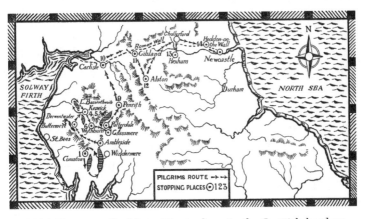

In 1801 Hutton walked from Birmingham to the Scottish borders and back when he was in his seventies.

to average a steady two and a half miles per hour. He expected to eat and drink where he could. 'An antiquary does not deserve the name who cannot fast half a day and live hard the other half.'

In 1801, shortly before his seventy-eighth birthday he walked out from his home at Bennett's Hill, bound for Penrith and Hadrian's Wall. It was the year when Ludwig van Beethoven was working on his *Moonlight Sonata* and a Mr Richard Trevithick was bolting together a contraption that would become the world's first pressure steam engine. In the English countryside, however, there was no rural Golden Age: Bonaparte's 'Frenchies' looked increasingly likely to invade and a succession of poor harvests and high bread prices bred poverty and suspicion in the normally peaceable shires. Hutton found himself taken for a spy, a government inspector, a quack doctor, his budget 'stuffed with laxatives', even, Heaven forbid, a Methodist preacher. Catherine, his daughter, insisted on accompanying him, riding ahead on horseback with their servant (she as his pillion-passenger) to arrange the night's lodgings. He would reach his destination having walked at his steady two and a half miles an hour, dine well and rise from his bed at four o'clock the following morning. When he broke for breakfast at an inn the solicitous Catherine would join him, pay the bill and ride on to the next night's rest.

At Penrith he would have no more of her company. Forbidding her to follow – she left to visit the Lake District – he journeyed on to the Wall where

Hadrian's Wall, where Hutton made his 'Mural Tournification'

he underwent an almost transcendental experience as he walked into view of the Wall: 'Unable to proceed,' he records: 'forgot I was upon a wild common, a stranger, and the evening approaching; lost in astonishment, I was not able to move at all.' But move he did, eventually.

Walking on alone (except for the companionship of his imaginary friends, Agricola, Severus and Hadrian himself) William Hutton performed the 'Mural Tourification', as the Rev'd John Lingard pompously described it six years later. He fell into good company and bad (at one point persuading a landowner to desist from stone robbing the wall for his farmhouse), and good beds and bad (at the Twice Brewed inn he encountered a rude party of carriers).

Over seven and a half days William Hutton traversed the wall from end to end.

'Perhaps I am the first man that ever travelled the whole length?' he mused. 'So long and solitary a journey was never performed by a man of seventy-eight. It has excited the curiosity of the town and causes me frequently to be stopped in the street.' Eventually he was reunited with Catherine and together they journeyed back to Birmingham, he a stone lighter and the family purse down by forty guineas. The weather was intensely hot, yet in thirty-five days, Hutton had walked 600 miles.

The Birmingham businessman who later published his account of pedestrian peregrinations in Wales, *Remarks upon North Wales*, being the result of *Sixteen tours through that part of the Principality* and the Scotland trip as *The History of the Roman Wall* continued to ramble until he could ramble no more. In 1813, on his ninetieth birthday, he walked ten miles. 'Every man has his hobby horse', he once declared. 'And I ride mine when I walk on foot.'

ELLEN WEETON
'I choose to ramble without restraint'

On Christmas Day 1776, while her father, Captain Thomas Weeton, was at sea aboard his privateer, *The Nelly*, Ellen Weeton was born in Lancaster. The child was named after the ship, an unfortunate reminder since her father died aboard it six years later, struck in the face by chain shot during an attack on an American ship. The captain's death presaged difficult times ahead for young Ellen Weeton.

Thomas Weeton's wife Mary, left alone to bring up Ellen and her son Thomas, set up a private school. Ellen worked there too, mother and daughter bound together in virtual slavery. When Mary died, her death said to have been brought on by the shock of being verbally abused by one of the parents, Ellen tried to run the school alone: she had to support her brother (who would eventually, and ungratefully, slander poor Ellen before being caught up in a corruption scandal).

Eventually Ellen gave up the school and for some years held a series of posts as governess until, rather suddenly, she announced to friend that she had accepted a proposal of marriage from one Aaron Stock of Wigan. (Was it unconnected with the fact that one of her charges had recently told her to her face that she was ugly?) But by the time they had one daughter, Mary, Aaron Stock had turned into 'a monster of a husband' who mocked his wife for her 'haggard countenance and skeleton figure'. He drove Ellen from the family home and separated her from her daughter. Faced with more misery and continued financial difficulties, Ellen Weeton would have led a sorry life, but for one consolation: she loved to walk. 'I chose to go alone, in places unfrequented by those of my own species, that my thoughts, as well as my feet, may ramble without restraint.'

She and her brother had walked Dean Wood, a

In the 1820s it was not seemly for a woman like Ellen Weeton to be walking for pleasure alone. *(Punch)*

local beauty spot near Upholland as children. She was happy to walk to visit her daughter when the girl attended boarding school in St Helens, seven miles away. During a brief stay in London in 1824, she walked everywhere she could, although she confessed that 'when I enter towns, and crowds, I do then like to have a companion'.

Walking saved paying stage coach fares and avoided the unwelcome attention of male passengers. On the journey to London she described the company of an Irishman 'his head likewise jolting against me perpetually. It was intolerable'. For Weeton, walking gave her the freedom to be who she was, to do as she liked and to enjoy those occasions 'when the wonders of nature alone occupy me, when my soul is filled with admiration and rapture at scenes of rural beauty'.

In 1825, aged forty-nine, she took to the 'mountainous grandeur' of North Wales with a walking tour that included an ascent of Snowdon and a twenty-five mile tramp in one day. In the nineteenth century it was not seemly for a woman to be walking alone for her pleasure. In Wales, as she wrote to a friend, 'I do certainly observe myself to be looked at more than I ever recollect before.' Was it, she mused, because she was ugly? 'I am taller and thinner than most women and very plain featured.' Was it her mode of dress which was 'very plain, that I may pass unnoticed; a dark print, no way remarkable in the make of it, and a bonnet likewise plain?' No. Above all it was that women did not do this kind of thing: and she knew it well: 'It is no very common thing, I suppose, to see strangers go up the mountains, particularly a decently dressed female, alone'.

Ellen Weeton died in relative obscurity in 1849. Ninety years later, when her *Journal of a Governess* was published, readers began to learn about, and like, this curious, early Victorian who triumphed over adversity by walking. For plain Miss Weeton was remarkable for her literary skills and her determination to exercise them. She had kept a detailed journal and from it sourced material for letters to friends and family. The letters themselves were no casual missives, dashed off between supper and sleep, but detailed descriptions of her life and her walks. And she wrote for prosterity the long letters apparently confident that her future readers would, one day, be following vicariously in her footsteps.

One of the best illustrations of her joyful walking was on 23 May in 1812 when she caught the boat, *Brilliant*, to the Isle of Man for a five week holiday. 'My walks during my residence in the Island, have been many and long,' she wrote in one of her 10,000 word letters, estimating that she had covered at least 203 miles on foot. She made her first walk, around thirteen miles, towards the mountains. She wore a grey stuff jacket, petticoat and a 'small slouch straw hat' and carried a parasol in one hand and, in the other, a white net bag containing her memorandum book and a map which she purchased so as to avoid having to ask directions. 'I took my guide in my hand, and wanted no other.'

Weeton experienced the familiar worries of the lone woman out walking. Her journeys were 'not without considerable apprehensions, lest I should meet with insult.' Women she finds are 'civil, humane, and hospitable, but of men I cannot say so; frequently, when I, or other females, have passed them, have I seen their sneers, or heard their rude remarks.' When on one walk she was overtaken by an Irishman she assessed the dangers before responding to his attempts at conversation reasoning that 'he was old, and rather infirm, and I was confident I could overpower him should he attempt to rob me.' At any rate, she thinks, she could outrun him. This was during an early walk when she covered thirteen miles and climbed Greeba. She noted with distress a young woman in bare feet gathering furze or heather for the fire. 'The tears in her eyes evinced the pains she felt. The poor women in the Island seldom wear shoes or stockings whilst the men seldom go without; why there should be such apparent injustice . . . I know not.'

Her next walk was a twelve mile tramp to Kirk-Santon. However she stretches it to sixteen 'as I seldom go directly on without swerving occasionally from the road.' Two days later she wanders off to Laxey past Kirk Conchan where the village boys are tolling the funeral bell. For a moment she thinks the village lads are jingling the bell 'instead of a frying pan, to ring a swarm of bees into a hive'. When a boy by the roadside puts her right she concludes: 'How careful should travellers be of . . . taking for reality, what only appears to be very probable. I walked on, laughing heartily at the idea.'

On her return she fell in with a peddler woman who offered to tell her fortune. 'I laughed and told her I dared not venture; for she could only tell me that I must die a miserable old maid.' The two part company, Ellen regretting the missed opportunity to discover 'the hope of a husband, and a fine coach, which might have cheered me even to my last moments. Goosecap! noodle! ninny hammer! no name is too bad for me!'

On 5 June she walks thirty five miles in a twelve

hour day, 'a tolerable journey, even for a horse.' Nearing four o'clock in the afternoon she faces the dilemma which every walker must face once in a while: whether to press on or to return. After brief hesitation she opts for the high, mountain road because 'I wanted scenery and prospect, not caring for the additional fatigue.' She is rewarded with clear views across the Irish Sea to England, Scotland and Wales, and to Ireland and the Mourne Mountains 'of a deep purple, tinged with the declining sun.' And she is justly proud of herself: 'to stand as I did, upon an island, and in half an hour see three kingdoms and a principality, is no common view.'

A few days later she walks another twenty two miles and later still another thirteen mile walk, always checking the distances on her map although she believes she has 'a tolerable idea' of how long it takes her to cover a mile. By now her feet are so badly blistered she is obliged to rest for several days.

She is soon on her feet again, this time with the summit of Snaefell, or 'Snafeld' (620 m), in her sights. Of all her ventures, the Isle of Man was the most rewarding. The weather had turned cold and misty as she set out and she wished she could postpone Snaefell for another day. But with too little time left of her holiday she must forge forward with 'a sort of irresistible impulse.' The wind picks up. It howls through the heather 'like the voice of a human being in distress'. When she reaches the summit it roars around her like a tempest. Struggling to fulfill the ritual of adding a stone to the summit's cairn she is blown over, but crawls on her hands and knees to add 'my mite to the heap.' The weather takes a turn for the worst and, as lowering cloud threatens to envelop the summit, she picks up her skirts and scampers down the hillside.

Resting by the skeleton of a sheep Ellen Weeton contemplates her own fate for a moment: 'I too, may die here, thought I. And, thinking how uncomfortable it would be to lie dead in such a place, unburied, my clothes battered off my body by the winds, my flesh pecked off by sea gulls, and my naked bone bleached by the weather till they were as white as those of the sheep, I heaved a sigh!'

Then she bursts into spontaneous laughter at her dark thoughts and we leave Ellen Weeton, the woman who walked away her unhappiness, as she returns to her lodgings 'feeling as little fatigue after a walk of 20 miles, as if I had scarcely walked four.'

Footnote: Bloomers

The invention of the liberating Bloomers walking costume was attributed to the newspaper proprietor Amelia Bloomer. In the mid 1800s, she wore nothing else. 'I found the dress comfortable, light, and convenient, and well adapted to the needs of my busy life. For some six or eight years . . . and until the papers had ceased writing squibs at my expense, I wore no other costume,' she wrote in later life.

Born in Cortland County, New York in 1818, Amelia Bloomer had edited a temperance paper called *Lily* in Seneca Falls. She regularly spoke on temperance and women's rights at public meetings and she constantly wore the dress with which her name was associated. But, as she herself wrote, 'nothing lies like history'.

The real story behind the invention of the bloomers was that a rival paper, the *Seneca County Courier* whose editor was opposed to women's rights, ran a satirising piece suggesting that suffragettes should wear pantaloons. Amelia Bloomer ran her own piece approving the idea. Shortly afterwards an emancipated young woman, Elizabeth Smith Miller, appeared on the streets in short skirts and full Turkish trousers – with the approval of her husband and her father, a US Congressman. Miller's cousin, Elizabeth Cady Stanton, followed suit with a black satin skirt that came a little below the knees and which was worn over trousers of the same material.

'A few days later I too donned the costume,' wrote Amelia Bloomer. 'I stood amazed at the furor I had unwittingly caused. Someone – I don't know to whom I am

Results of Bloomerism (*Punch*)

A poser for a Bloomer (*Punch*)

indebted for the honor – wrote of the "Bloomer costume," and the name has continued to cling to the short
dress in spite of my repeatedly disclaiming all right to it
and giving Mrs. Miller's name as the originator.'

Even as the British and American press mocked the
shameless costume, the circulation of Amelia Bloomer's
magazine soared as women across the country sought out
patterns for making their own bloomers. Yet many women
had misgivings about the modern dress. According to
the Liberator magazine (August 1851) a woman at a
party attacked another who was wearing bloomers for
her immodesty. Her neighbour retorted: 'If you pull your
dress up enough to cover your shoulders it would then
be shorter than mine'. The lady fainted into a lemonade
waiter.

GEORGE BORROW
'Robbers never carry umbrellas'

With a soldier for a father and an actress for a
mother, George Borrow, born on 5 July 1803, might
have expected to have had an unusual childhood.
He was, certainly, an unusual boy. He was thirteen
when his family, often pressed for funds, finally settled in Norwich after constantly moving from one
army barracks to another. George promptly went off
to play with the Gypsies and quickly picked up the
Romany *cant*. He had a natural talent for languages
and was said to have mastered twelve by the age of
eighteen.

George Borrow, able to walk 'in the genuine Barclay fashion' if the need arose.

'I picked up some Latin and Greek at school; some Irish in Ireland and . . . have learned some Welsh partly from books and partly from a Welsh groom,' he revealed in *Wild Wales*, his account of a walk through the principality in 1854.

'The inhabitants . . . call their country *Cymru*. Wales or Walia, however, is the true, proper, and without doubt original name,' he wrote in his introduction, demonstrating his linguistic knowledge as he listed the origins of the word Wales in Balkan, Anglo-Saxon, English, Old English, Celtic, 'Cumbric', Sanskrit and German. ('The original name of Italy, (is) still called by the Germans Welschland.') He accepted that he was making some 'startling assertions', but did not doubt that they would be 'universally acknowledged' some time in the future. This is the essential Borrow, a man with absolute faith in his own judgement.

Wild Wales was published in 1862, eight years after the walk itself, and based upon the notebooks he made at the time. Comparing the details in *Wild Wales* with the often sparse notebook entries, Borrow either possessed a prodigious memory, or a highly creative imagination. Or both.

By the time of his fifty-first birthday, the year of his Welsh walk, Borrow had spent ten years travelling through Europe and Russia with the British and Foreign Bible Society. (He had secured the job in the first place by walking from Norfolk to London, a distance of 112 miles, in twenty seven hours.) Borrow had, by now, written the best seller which earned him most of his money, *The Bible in Spain*, and two works on the lives of Gypsies, *Lavengro and The Romany Rye*. And he had inherited, or acquired, a list of prejudices which would have qualified him as the author of quarrelsome letters to The Times on any subject from antislavery, Catholicism and industrialism, to the railways, Victorian manners or cruelty to animals. ('I . . . am silly enough to feel disgust and horror at the squeals of a rat in the fangs of a terrier,' he admitted once.) Yet he remains a likeable and entertaining walking author. As Hugh Oliffe puts it in *On Borrow's Trail* (2003): 'I like him because he is quite simply the liveliest of writers on Wales.'

Wild Wales earned the author little during his lifetime, but eventually sold well and survives still as an engaging account of a long hike through Wales. The tour, apparently, was prompted by boredom. 'We are a country people in a corner of East Anglia, and . . . had been residing so long in our own little estate, that we had become tired of the objects around us, and conceived that we should be all the better for changing the scene for a short period.'

His wife Mary proposed Harrowgate or Leamington. Borrow insisted upon Wales 'more especially as I was acquainted with the Welsh language'. Consequently he, Mary and his step daughter Henrietta boarded the train for Chester on 27 July 1854.

His love of *Cymraeg* is a constant theme in *Wild Wales*. At one point a woman tells him she thought it physically impossible for an Englishman to speak Welsh; at another a young carter explains that he swears at his horses in English since 'Welsh isn't strong enough.' Walking to Beddgelert from Bangor he pauses for refreshments at an inn and buys the postman a whisky. The postie, glass in hand, foolishly begins to mock Borrow in Welsh to his companions. Too late does the landlady warn the postman that her guest 'has the language': Borrow looks the startled postie in the eye and tells him: '*dwy o iaith dwy o wyneb*: two languages, two faces, friend!' And bidding the company good evening strides triumphantly out into the night.

Borrow began his walking tour by sending his family ahead on the train from Chester to Llangollen and following behind on foot 'as by walking I should be better able to see the country than by making the journey by the flying vehicle.' Covering the 20 miles he questions passers-by in their mother tongue. One after another replies politely in English. Then he hears 'dim saesneg' (no English) from a woman walking to Rhiwabon. Now he can truthfully say: 'I

Borrow admired the ruins
of the Cistercian
abbey, Vale Crucis, near
Llangollen. (Arkitype)

am in Wales.'

Having settled the family at Llangollen, Borrow
warms up with a few short walks in the district. He
notes slate, destined for Paddington's housing boom,
being loaded on to barges on the canal, and wanders
up to the ruins of Vale Crucis, the ruined Cistercian
abbey, outside the town. A few days later he passes
the abbey again, this time on a more ambitious
tramp to Ruthin with a guide, John Jones. He and
Jones covered the distance in 15 hours including a
walk over the dramatic Horseshoe Pass. 'It took us
a long time to get to the top', wrote Borrow adding
that the countryside reminded him of Spain.

Now he is ready for some serious walking. He

leaves for Bangor 'on foot in order that I might have perfect liberty of action and enjoy the best opportunities of seeing the country.' (He leaves on a Sunday in order to observe what the Welsh do on the Sabbath and is himself criticised for breaking the day of rest 'by idly walking about.') He reached Bangor in two days and went on to tour Anglesey, in his view the Isle of Poets and the cause of some unfortunate confusion. Seeking a publican who is reputed to be a great poet he mistakenly calls at the wrong inn. 'Has your master written any poetry?' he asks the serving girl.

'No, sir,' replies the shocked girl. 'My master is a respectable man and would scorn to do anything of that kind.'

Borrow is a master of anecdote, even when the tale is told against himself. Deep in the North Welsh mountains, for example, he meets a man with a dog called Perro. He is curious to know why the man should call his pet by the Spanish word for dog. 'We call him Perro,' explains the man patiently, 'because he is called Perro.'

Borrow, like Ellen Weeton almost thirty years earlier, is bowled over by the scenery. Beaumaris Bay is 'far superior' to the bay at Naples, Llyn Cwellyn, the 'silver lake and the shadowy mountain' make for 'a world of wonder' while the Snowdon mountain range is 'one of the most romantic'. He scales Snowdon, or Yr Wyddfa, with his daughter in four hours and is rewarded with fine weather on the summit. 'There we stood on the Wyddfa, in a cold bracing atmosphere, though the day was almost stiflingly hot in the regions from which we had ascended'. They gaze out on Wales, 'a part of Cumberland; the Irish Channel, and what might be either a misty creation or the shadowy outline of the hills of Ireland.' Borrow feels inspired to declaim a few lines of Welsh poetry much to the amusement of some English gentleman who are sharing the summit. Borrow descends, ashamed of his countrymen.

He was anything but embarrassed about his abilities as a walker. On an eleven-day, 140 mile tramp from Bangor to Llangollen by way of Beddgelert, the Aberglaslyn Pass, Ffestiniog and Bala, he bristles at the suggestion that he is dragging his feet when a slate miner from Blaenau Ffestiniog notes that he walked very slowly. 'I am not in the slightest degree tired,' protests Borrow. 'Ah', remarks the old man laconically: 'Anybody can get along over level ground.' (After the weekend the Blaenau miners were in the habit of returning to work by running to the mines.)

Borrow meets his match when he encounters a 'tremendous' walker heading for Bangor market with his wares. The two stride out side by side in silence for some time until Borrow accelerates 'in genuine Barclay fashion' to overtake the man and bid him good evening face to face. They proceed in a friendly fashion to Bangor where he parts company 'with the kind six-mile-an-hour market-gardener.'

At the end of October 1854 Mary and Henrietta returned home. Borrow had his shoes resoled, his

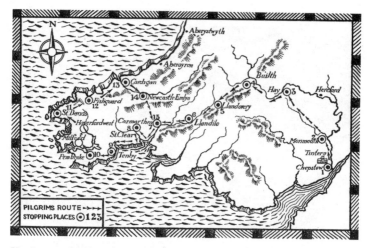

Having resoled his shoes and repaired his umbrella, Borrow toured South Wales on foot.

trusty umbrella repaired and, with twenty sovereigns in his purse, made tracks for a three-week walk through south Wales. He tramped on through Llanrhaedr-ym-Mochnant, Llansilin, Machynlleth and Devil's Bridge. He was led up Plynlimon to see the source of the Wye and Severn before returning to 'a capital supper.' How one enjoys one's supper after a good day's walk provided you can afford to pay the next day', he muses.

Borrow travelled on to Tregaron, reaching the town in the dark and completing the final miles under moonlight with a retired drover, before walking on through Llanddewi-Brefi, Llampeter, Llandovery ('the pleasantest little town'), Brynaman, Swansea, Neath, Newport and Chepstow. Ceremoniously drinking from the river Wye, just as he had done so

THE PIC-NIC.

Contented Man (loq.). "WHAT A NICE DAMP PLACE WE HAVE SECURED; AND HOW VERY FORTUNATE WE ARE IN THE WEATHER; IT WOULD HAVE BEEN SO PROVOKING FOR US ALL TO HAVE BROUGHT OUR UMBRELLAS AND THEN TO HAVE HAD A FINE DAY!! GLASS OF WINE, BRIGGS, EH?"

The umbrella, essential equipment except when the rain was in the face. *(Punch)*

at the source of the river on Plynlimon he washes it down with a bottle of port and departs for London having walked 'about 250 miles'. As his coach trundled back to London he could reflect once again on the 'oak-covered tops' of the hills, the mountains gilded in sunshine and the silvered waters of the Rheidol cataract. 'Should I live a hundred years I shall never forget the wild fantastic beauty of that morning scene.'

Borrow continued to take walking tours: the Isle of Man in 1855, a second walk of 400 miles through south, west and central Wales in 1857, and Scotland in 1858. (Presumably he had by then amended his views, expressed to a Durham miner in *Wild Wales*, that 'a queerer set of people than the Scotch you would scarcely see in a summer's day'). He walked the Scottish lowlands and tramped through Sussex and Hampshire. Even in his seventies, he not only walked, but, in winter, would break the ice and take a swim in the chilly Norfolk waters, running around naked afterwards in order to dry himself.

Borrow's greatest aid on these endeavours and his journeys through wild Wales was his umbrella, for him 'a tent, a shield, a lance, and a voucher for good character'. Returning to Bala across the moors on the first leg of his Welsh journey, for example, he is caught in a shower. Normally he does not 'care much for a wetting provided I have a good roof, a good fire, and good fare to betake myself to afterwards', but on this occasion having 'expanded my umbrella' he flung it over his shoulder and laughed.

An umbrella, Borrow explained, was everything the seasoned walker needed 'except when the rain is in his face.' Armed with an umbrella the pedestrian had no cause to fear wild bulls, ferocious dogs or footpads demanding money. Furthermore any landlord would recognise a man as being respectable if he had an umbrella; and no wanderer on the way would think twice about entering in to conversation with a traveller who carried an umbrella since 'robbers never carry umbrellas'.

ROBERT LOUIS STEVENSON
'I travel not to go anywhere, but to go'

'Every book is, in an intimate sense, a circular letter
to the friends of him who writes it. The public is but
a generous patron who defrays the postage.' So wrote
Robert Louis Stevenson to his friend Sidney Colvin
in 1876. And it was to Colvin that he dedicated
his second book, *Travels with a Donkey*, published
that year. He might as easily have signed it over to
his new lover, Mrs Fanny Osborne, or the one he
had most recently betrayed on a walk through the
Cevennes, Modestine.

Modestine was an ass. She walked at no more
than two miles an hour in all the 120 mile journey
from Le Monastier, fifteen miles from Le Puy to St
Jean du Gard. At the outset relations between man
and beast were cold: 'She was only an appurtenance
of my mattress, or self-acting bedstead on four cas-
tors.' Eleven days later she eats out of his hand 'for
she had a soft affection for me which I was soon to
betray.' Finally when, twelve days later, Modestine
was delivered to a new owner, saddle and all, for
thirty-five francs, Stevenson wept for his loss. 'She
was patient, elegant in form, the colour of an ideal
mouse, and inimitably small. Her faults were those
of her race and sex; her virtues were her own,' he
reflected as he rode off in the coach towards Alais
and a longed-for reunion with Fanny Osborne.

Thomas and Margaret Stevenson had christened
their only son Robert Lewis in 1850. The boy would

The 'idle child', Robert Louis Stevenson, walked 'for travel's sake'.
(Mary Evans Picture Library)

be a deep disappointment to his father. The last in the
line of three generations of swashbuckling engineers
who built and managed lighthouses for the Board of
Northern Lights and who made safe the shipping lanes
of New Zealand, Japan and India, Stevenson was sent
to study engineering at Edinburgh University in 1867.
The seventeen year old truanted from his lectures. 'I
was known and pointed out as an idler, and yet I was
always busy on my private end, which was to learn to
write,' wrote Stevenson in his own defence.

Stevenson had endured a sickly and isolated childhood. Chronic bronchitis kept him from school and
every winter his mother whisked him away from the
chills of their Scottish home to the kinder climates
of Italy, France, Germany and even Torquay. In his

loneliness the boy read, fuelling the imagination which, one day, would create Victorian best sellers such as *Treasure Island, Dr Jekyll and Mr Hyde* and *Kidnapped.*

Never guessing his son's latent talent, but realising that the boy would never make an engineer, Thomas Stevenson withdrew him from Edinburgh and sent him to London to study law. The callow youth simply ignored his studies, struck up a friendship with Sidney Colvin, then Slade Professor of Fine Arts, and spent months in France with Colvin and his wife. He also changed his name from the Protestant Lewis to the *louché* Louis – he was never known as Robert – and succeeded in publishing his first work, an essay entitled Roads, in Portfolio magazine. Stevenson senior was forced to acquiesce to his obdurate son and in 1875 he settled a small allowance on Louis. The young man left for France where he settled to write in the company of fellow artists living outside Paris in Barbizon in the Forest of Fountainbleu.

But what to write? Searching for source material he decided to journey on foot and by canoe along the rivers and canals that ran from Antwerp in Belgium to Pontoise in France, with friend Walter Simpson. The journey ended prematurely with Stevenson's arrest: the gendarmerie took him first for a seller of dubious literature and then more seriously as a spy and he was hauled before the local magistrate to explain himself. Failing to provide a convincing explanation Stevenson was expelled from the town. By now, however, he had gathered enough material for his first book, *An Inland Voyage* which was published in 1877.

When he returned to Barbizon to write the book he met a new addition to their bohemian set: Mrs Fanny Osborne. Mrs Osborne had left a husband in America and decamped to Fontainbleu with her two children. Stevenson was twenty-six, she was ten years older. Apart from the occasional break, the couple were destined to stay together for the rest of Stevenson's relatively short life.

The first of these occasional breaks came two years later when Stevenson travelled to Le Monastier and after a month's preparation, which included purchasing Modestine, walked out with her one October morning. In his book, *Travels with a Donkey*, Stevenson set out his philosophy on walking: 'I travel not to go anywhere, but to go. I travel for travel's sake. The great affair is to move; to come down off the feather-bed of civilisation, and find the globe granite underfoot and strewn with cutting flints.' He was being a little economical with the truth for he also travelled to write. Arriving at the prettily-named monastery of Our Lady of the Snows during the journey he confesses as much to a friar. He is, he admits, a literary man.

'Might I not introduce you as a geographer instead?' asks the friar hopefully.

'No', replies Stevenson, mindful of the truth.

'Very well then (with disappointment) an author.'

He is called upon to account for his literary ambitions again when he spent the night at an unpretentious auberge in Bouchet St Nichols, sharing his bedroom with a young man, his wife and child ('I know nothing of the woman except that she had beautiful arms, and seemed no whit embarrassed'). The living quarters were so small 'Modestine and I could hear each other dining'. Learning of his plans to write a travel book the landlady instructs him on what to include: '"Whether people harvest or not at such or such a place; if there were forests; studies of manners; what, for example, I and the master of the house say to you; the beauties of Nature, and all that.' He is compelled to agree with her. She turns to her husband, a simple man: 'You see,' she tells him triumphantly: 'I understood that.'

It proved to be good counsel. Generations of readers have since taken vicarious pleasure in Stevenson's account of a walk through the harshly beautiful countryside of the Cevennes, an account which documents the highs, lows and plateaus of a good, long tramp.

One of the Stevenson's preoccupations, and one that concerns any walker on a long journey, was where to rest one's head at night. Stevenson, like De Qunicey, devised his own piece of equipment for sleeping out. But while De Quincey came up with a prototype for the one-person tent, Stevenson invented the bivvybag, 'a sort of long roll or sausage, green waterproof cart-cloth without and blue sheep's fur within.' In fact Stevenson's may not have been the first bivvybag. Ronald Turnbull in *The Book of the Bivvy* reveals how the explorer Charles Packe, backpacking in the high

Pyrenees in 1858 had slept out in his sleeping bag. Meanwhile mystic Scottish Highlanders needing to gain a glimpse of the future were, according to Sir Walter Scott's *The Lady of the Lake*, wrapped in a crude bivvybag made from the bloodied hide of a fresh-slain bullock and left in some auspicious place overnight. (Turnbull is a great exponent of the bivvybag. 'People who don't smoke or drink also tend to have sexual intercourse less often. And I suspect, though this has not been studied by sociologists, that they tend to prefer the Pennines to the Isle of Skye and the B&B to the bivvybag.') Stevenson's fur-lined, canvass bivvybag, which doubled as a carry case during the day (its contents included an egg beater and a revolver) was so comfortable that he found himself longing for his 'sheepskin sac . . . and the lee of some great wood' during one teeth-chatteringly cold night in the public bedroom of a hotel.

Yet his first night in his bivvybag was not exactly relaxing. He pitched up in a black forest, a gale roaring through the trees, and, having tethered and fed Modestine, crawled inside, leaving his wet boots wrapped up in his waterproofs. Arranging his possessions close at hand and using his knapsack as a pillow he settled down for a cold supper of tinned Bologna sausage and a cake of chocolate washed down with neat brandy, 'a revolting beverage in itself'. After smoking 'one of the best cigarettes in my experience' he pulls the flap of his fur cap over his neck and eyes, places his revolver by his side 'and snuggled well down among the sheepskins.'

Stevenson spent the comfortably restless night that is familiar to anyone who sleeps beneath the stars. He concludes: 'I was surprised to find how easy and pleasant it had been, even in this tempestuous weather.' While his feet must find a place among the litter at the bottom of the bivvybag ('the lantern or the second volume of Peyrat's *Pastors in the Desert*') he awoke with 'not a touch of cold, and awakened with unusually lightsome and clear sensations.'

After his twelve day tramp through the Cevennes, Louis Stevenson would camp out no more. He went home to complete *Travels with a Donkey* while Fanny returned to America to arrange for her divorce. In 1880 he left Scotland to join her. They married and settled in California where the climate was kinder to his asthmatic condition. In the next six years Stevenson completed many of the books (including *Treasure Island, Dr Jekyll and Mr Hyde* and *Kidnapped*) which earned him enough to buy an estate in Apia, Samoa. He died there on 3 December 1894 and was buried on the summit of Pala Mountain.

HILAIRE BELLOC
'It's only the first step that counts'

Hilaire Belloc, born at Saint-Cloud in France to an English mother and a French father, studied at Balliol College, Oxford in the days when many a tutor regarded a daily constitutional as essential exercise for the literary mind. Belloc, with a literary life ahead of him as essayist, historian, novelist and poet, responded by undertaking a series of long walks: to Holyhead, York and, in a record time of eleven and a half hours, to London's Marble Arch from Oxford's Carfax.

But he honed his walking style in 1901 with a purposeful, 700 mile wander through Europe, starting at Toul in Moselle (as a Frenchman, he had served his military training here) and finishing at St. Peter's in Rome. He aimed to cover thirty miles a day, to walk all the way and 'take advantage of no wheeled thing', to sleep under the stars and to hear Mass (he was a faithful Catholic) at St Peter's on the Feast of Saints Peter and Paul. And he broke most of his own promises, often lodging in pensionnes and frequently hopping on the back of a passing peasant's cart. He did, however, pen the best motto for a walker – 'It's only the first step that counts' – and he reached Rome in time for mass (although he heard it in a different church) and returned to write up the notes of his journey in *The Path to Rome*, published in 1902.

He judged *The Path to Rome* a 'jolly book' to write, and the reading public, their appetite whetted for long distance walking stories by Stevenson's *Travels with a Donkey* published twenty years earlier, found it a jolly book to read. *The Path to Rome* turned into a profitable best seller and made the author a respected walking writer.

Belloc travelled light, wearing a white linen suit and a jaunty straw hat and carrying a sturdy walking stick and a canvass satchel. It contained very little: a sketchbook and some pencils, some food and 'a quart of the wine of Brulé', a needle and thread, a cup and a flute. There was no change of clothes, no raincoat and no sleeping bag. (Wiser in his old age he later offered walkers stern words of advice in *The Pyrenees* published in 1909, about taking proper clothes and sleeping sacks.) His first night in the open, tucked up in a haystack, convinced Belloc to seek the home comforts of an inn for most of the twenty-six nights it took him to cover the 700 miles. (For five nights of the journey he walked from dusk to dawn, sleeping in the heat of the day instead.)

Belloc had devised the route to Rome by drawing a straight line down the map and then adapting it to the local topography. Inevitably he made mistakes. Trying to cross into Italy on his chosen route over the Gries Pass he was overtaken by a blizzard and found himself looking 'over an awful gulf at great white fields of death'. Belloc, although he was moved by the sight of Alps, was no mountaineer and ill-equipped in his linen suit and straw hat. He had to be led back to safety by a local guide. The next day he crossed by the Gotthard Pass gazing up great clouds which 'I worshipped . . . so far as it is permitted to worship inanimate things,' wrote the good Catholic.

For his next long distance walk Belloc, in 1904, took to a trail that was already well established, The Pilgrims' Way, linking the cathedrals of Winchester and Canterbury. The ecclesiastical definition of a

Hilaire Belloc started
his walking career as an
Oxford undergraduate.
(Mary Evans Picture Library)

pilgrimage is a journey to a chosen shrine of at least ninety three miles (150 km): at 129 miles (192 km) the Pilgrims' Way made for a perfect pilgrimage. Avoiding the exposed ridge of the North Downs, the Pilgrims' Way ran along its warmer, southern slopes while keeping to the terraces above the sticky Wealden clay at the foot of the ridge. Today the Way trips over motorways and stumbles past gentrified farmhouses, but in 1904 it was a greener and more tranquil path. Walking it gave Belloc the opportunity to 'forget the vileness of my own time and renew for some few days the better freedom of that vigorous morning when men were erect, articulate, and worshipping God, but not yet broken by complexity and the long accumulation of evil.'

The Way led to the place where Saint Thomas á Becket was murdered at Canterbury Cathedral in 1170. Parts of the Way received the stamp of offi-

The Pilgrim's Way

aldom eight hundred years later when Becket's successor, Donald Coggan, Archbishop of Canterbury, opened the North Downs Way, the national trail from Farnham to Dover.

Becket had been slain by knights loyal to King Henry II, responding to the king's call to be rid of 'this troublesome priest'. Within a year there were rumours that fourteen people had received miraculous cures at the priest's shrine. Soon pilgrims' ways were radiating out from Canterbury like the wheel spokes on a brewer's dray, with the faithful trudging out of Dover, Southampton and London as well as Winchester to walk (and even crawl the final stretch) to Canterbury. Inn keepers, shoemakers and souvenir sellers were quick to set up their stalls along the routes.

Why Winchester should have come to regard their

path to Canterbury as the one and only Pilgrims'
Way is a minor mystery. It was partly a result of
some mediaeval tourist promotion. At the time of
Becket's death the Exchequer had packed up and
moved out of Winchester, the nation's old capital,
to be near the new law courts in the new capital,
London. Winchester's aldermen were more than
happy to contend that their Way was The Way and
cash in on the pilgrims' pennies. Yet as late as 1860
there was nothing on the map to identify this as a significant religious thoroughfare. The route, although
it has inspired and moved many a Christian, may
have been committed to paper by an anonymous
civil servant who, in his best italic script, chose to
add the words Pilgrims' Way when new maps were
drawn up.

In fact the Pilgrims' Way was a thoroughfare
long before Henry's hit men did for Becket. Belloc
had a great respect for such ancient roads, 'the most
imperative and the first of our necessities', and which
he regarded as a 'supreme collective endeavour'. But
Belloc was intent on following, literally, in the footsteps of the early pilgrims and so set off, not on some
fine, spring morning, but on the day of Thomas á
Becket's murder, 29 December. He and his companion carried no packs, averaged eighteen or so miles
a day and stayed overnight in local lodgings. Now,
as he forgot the vileness of his time, he concentrated
on the factual details of what he called his 'historical
essay' as he mapped out the old road. Curiously the
moralistic Belloc who went on to become a Liberal

Member of Parliament and a scholarly biographer (and who carried out much of his research on foot) was not above a little larceny. At one point he and his companion, their way obstructed by the river Wey, resorted to stealing a boat and, using his walking stick as a paddle, sculled across the other side where they landed to the sound of violent protest from the boat's owner on to the opposite bank. Perhaps it was not such a surprise. After his death the high-minded Catholic would be remembered less for his long walks than for having created that lying little minx, Matilda in *Cautionary Tales*.

WILLIAM HUDSON
'A traveller in little things'

William Henry Hudson was a strange individual. He wandered rather than strode around the English shires in the early 1900s, his wife, his 'snail in a woman shape' trailing behind, as he collected anecdotes and observations for his book, *Afoot in England*, published in 1908. After the bombast of Taylor and Borrow, the private pleasures of Ellen Weeton, Hutton's stolid pedestrianism and the professional story telling of Stevenson and Belloc, Hudson is the quiet and intro-spective walking writer.

Afoot in England was, he explained in the introduc-tion, 'a poor pedestrian's unimportant impressions of places and faces'. (All these p's came by accident, he apologised, recalling the editor who solemnly told

A cycling club circa 1900. Hudson was as happy on his bike as he was one his own two feet. (Herefordshire Lore)

him that 'he couldn't abide and wouldn't have alliteration's artful aid in his periodical.') Yet the novelist John Galsworthy praised the author for taking readers on a tour into 'a rare, free natural world'.

Born in Buenos Aires in 1841 to an American farming family, Hudson learned more from roaming the pampas and observing the birds than he did from any formal schooling. In 1869, after an illness that left him permanently debilitated, and a bout of depression which made him the cold, sober individual he was, Hudson emigrated to England.

For the next thirty years he and his wife, who ran a boarding house, lived a life of penury while he worked as a writer, astonished by his own admission when an article sent to a magazine earned 'a cheque worth several pounds'. Foggy London, much as he detested it, was the only place 'where our poor talents could earn us a few shillings a week to live on,' he wrote in 1902. Even as he penned these words his *Green Mansions* was about to be published to some critical acclaim. His tale of a haunting bird-girl caught the attention of literary contemporaries including Galsworthy and Joseph Conrad. Hudson continued to write until ill health finally defeated him. He died in 1922.

But for the present, 1903, 'on account of poverty and ill health', he and his wife could afford a short walking (sometimes cycling) tour, two or three times a year. They made an odd couple, he abandoning her on the road to 'force my way through unkempt hedges, climb hills, and explore woods and thickets'. Yet he was a poor walker himself and after his forays to 'converse with every bird and shy little beast and scaly creature I could discover' (he was a close observer of the natural world) he would return to his wife's side. She, 'slower than the proverbial . . . tortoise', then slackened her own pace to keep him company and together they would seek lodgings for the night. Since their funds did not extend very far, they laid up with cottagers, poorer than themselves, but, in those days, glad of a shilling or two.

Unlike Borrow, Stevenson or Belloc, Hudson laid no cartographer's trail for readers to follow (the couple walked without guidebooks or maps). He rarely gave

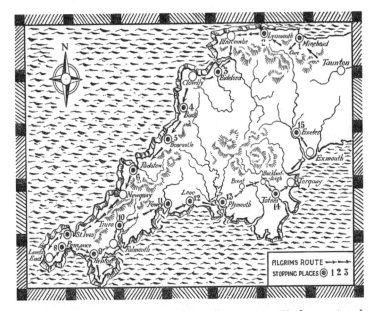

Although vague about many of his walking routes, Hudson enjoyed
the shires of Devon and Cornwall.

the location of his encounters and often disguised
them: 'I came by chance to the village – Norton,
we will call it, just to call it something'. Instead he
used his hiking days as an opportunity to minutely
observe the country people of England going about
their business.

In Wiltshire a 'handsome young woman' refuses
payment for lodgings and tells him: 'We all have
enough'. On the Norfolk coast the 'large English
blondes . . . tall and large in every way, very white-
skinned, with light or golden hair and large high-
blue eyes' congregate at the seaside like 'a herd of
large beautiful white cows.' A cowman he meets as

he tramps towards Ottery St Mary in Devon has a shapeless nose, grizzled beard and ears 'like the handles of a rudely shaped terracotta vase'. Yet 'though Nature had made him ugly, he had an agreeable expression, a sweet benign look in his large dark eyes, which attracted me, and I stayed to talk with him.'

His observations of wildlife, and British birds especially, is precise and poetic as he celebrates the 'loneliness and isolation underlying our pleasure in nature when walking'. In Norfolk he marvels at the tormented and crazed swifts and 'the fury that possessed them'. At night under the moon in an orchard he listens to the reeling of nightjars and after a moment 'that powerful melody that in its purity and brilliance invariably strikes us with surprise,' the song of the nightingale. Walking the coast east of Branscombe in Devon provides him with hours of 'rare happiness' watching motionless herring-gulls on the rocks like the 'sculpted figures of angels and saintly men and women . . . placed in niches of a cathedral front.'

On one walk Hudson has a bizarre encounter with a south Devon clergyman who had persuaded a local worthy to sponsor a new church. This was so that the priest could be rid of the toads in the old church that used to emerge from under the damp flags of the old building church to be fed titbits by his flock as he sermonised from the pulpit.

Hudson was, in his own words, one of the 'travellers in little things', but the wider picture of English

Afoot in England, William Hudson portrayed some of the hard realities of English country life.

country life did not escape him. With cheap imports of North American wheat, and high levels of emigration to Canada, New Zealand and Australia (anywhere but class-ridden Britain) the countryside was bleeding to death. When he and his wife stayed with a Mrs Flowerdew and her four young children in their vine-clad cottage, the woman's neighbours lend her the wherewithal – a roll of bedding, cane chairs, basin, ewer and floor mats – since the bailiffs had removed her furniture. He could not know that the young boys who with a great shout of excited joy 'rush pell-mell forth and scatter about the village' would, within eleven years, be fed to the fire fight on the Western Front. But he was keenly aware of the pious hypocrisy of the times when a country girl could, turning tricks for sailors, earn twice in a night what she could earn in a week as a between stairs maid. He observed the ladies of one parish, wearing egret and bird-of-paradise 'plums' in their bonnets, break bread and take wine 'in remembrance of an event supposed to be of importance to their souls'.

Hudson slipped into another angry reverie when, walking to find the site of a lost Roman town, *Calleva*, he finds himself trespassing in a 'sacred pheasant reserve'. He rehearses what he will say if he meets the landowner's 'sour faced gamekeeper with the cold blue unfriendly eyes . . . gun in hand to hear my excuses for trespassing. I should say (mentally): This man is distinctly English, and his far off progenitors, somewhere about sixteen hundred years ago probably assisted at the massacre of the pleasant little city at my feet.'

He was the arch exponent of the chance discovery. In rambling, insists Hudson, the charm of the unknown is paramount. 'If I have a purpose in this book, which is without a purpose . . . (it is) the infinitely greater pleasure in discovering the interesting things for ourselves than in informing ourselves of them by reading.'

CHAPTER 5

A Walk on the Wild Side

LESLIE STEPHEN

'Delicious bits of walking . . . await the man who
has no superstitious reverence for legal rights'

Born in 1832, Leslie Stephen was, during his seventy
two years, a Cambridge tutor, journalist, editor of
the Dictionary of National Biography ('that damned
Dictionary' as he called it) and an Alpine climber. He
counted Charles Darwin, T.H. Huxley, George Eliot and
Henry James among his acquaintances. He helped the
young Robert Louis Stevenson become a published
writer, and he married Minny, the daughter of the
Victorian novelist William Makepeace Thackeray.
Following her death and his subsequent marriage to
Julia Duckworth he fathered two of the most significant voices in the Bloomsbury set, Vanessa, later Bell,

and her younger sister, Virgina, later Woolf.

He was a respectable member of the Victorian literary establishment: he was, after all, knighted by Queen Victoria. He was also a domestic tyrant, prone to particular rages when, on Wednesdays, the housekeeping accounts were formally presented for his approval and the signing of the weekly household cheque. When he worked, according to Virginia, he did so sunk in a low rocking chair, smoking a clay pipe and scattering books around him in a circle, the thud of books hitting the floor resounding around the house. He continued to write in his final years although he became increasingly deaf and eccentric. Despite his position in society and his prodigious output as a Victorian writer he was largely remembered, after his death from cancer in 1904, for his work on the *National Dictionary of Biography*, and as the father of the two Bloomsbury women. Virginia Woolf is said to have portrayed him as Mr Ramsay in her novel *To The Lighthouse*: 'petty, selfish, vain, egotistical; he is spoilt; he is a tyrant; he wears Mrs Ramsay to death'.

Stephen considered most of his magazine writing as lightweight, yet he penned a significant piece on the pleasures of walking in *Studies of a Biographer* (1902). And when what he called a 'penny-a-liner in some obscure paper' quoted from the article, *In Praise of Walking*, and described him as 'the most loved of all men of letters, Stephen was flattered and wrote to his sister-in-law, Mary Fisher, to tell her so. For Leslie Stephen was an enthusiastic walker. ('Hurrah. I shall go out for a walk,' he wrote to a friend on completion of yet another tedious magazine piece). Stephen was also among the first to found one of those curious British collectives, the walking club.

When Stephen went up to Trinity Hall, Cambridge there was already a well established tradition amongst certain academics and their undergraduates for taking a hike. It persisted in 1913 when George Macaulay Trevelyan published his *Clio: A Muse and other essays*. An academic looking for a real pedestrian challenge could, wrote Trevelyan, try walking the eighty miles between the St Mary College in Oxford and the St Mary's in Cambridge within twenty-four hours. He also recommended that the aspiring Oxford or Cambridge man mark up his personal best, at a speed which would do credit to his college, by walking from either city to Marble Arch in London as Belloc had done. When walking from Cambridge to Marble Arch, Trevelyan suggested starting after breakfast at five in the morning and ordering a second breakfast to be ready at Royston by eight o'clock. Stephen knew the route well enough. He once walked from Cambridge to London . . . to attend a dinner party.

If senior establishment figures in the early twentieth century preferred the golf links and grouse moors, in the 1890s they were just as likely to be hiking around the green lanes of the Home Counties. Walking was healthy (Trevelyan reported that he had two doctors: his left leg and his right), virtuous and exclusive. 'When you have made an early start, followed the coastguard track . . . and at last

Walking clubs became a feature of English country life in the
1900s. (Herefordshire Lore)

emerged upon a headland where you can settle in to
a nook of the rocks . . . then you can consume your
modest sandwiches, light your pipe, and feel more
virtuous and thoroughly at peace with the universe,'
wrote Stephen in *In Praise of Walking*. Tramps like
these made one feel like 'a felicitous blend of poet and
saint', a sensation, he reminded his readers, that was
confined to the walker alone.

In October 1879 Stephen founded a fortnightly
walking club, the Sunday Tramps and he led its members on their first hike, to Richmond, the following
month. He continued to lead the Sunday Tramps for
the next twelve years and to accompany them for
another three years as they hiked through the lanes
and byways of Kent and Surrey. Such was the high-
brow nature of the conversation on these walks that

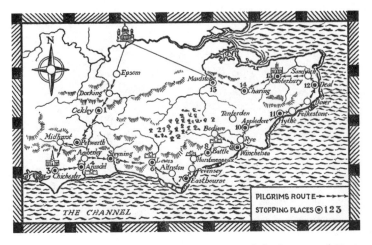

Leslie Stephen's Sunday walking group tramped the byways of Kent and Surrey.

one member of the 'Order of Sunday Trampers', the novelist George Meredith, voiced the opinion that, for the sake of the nation, they should be accompanied by a shorthand writer.

One constant topic of conversation was the frequent signs forbidding entry to this or that path. Keep Out. Trespassers prosecuted. Private Land. Stephen actively sought them out. 'They gave a strong presumption that the trespass must have some attraction,' he declared. 'To me it was a reminder of the many delicious bits of walking which, even in the neighbourhood of London, await the man who has no superstitious reverence for legal rights.'

Signs which promised to prosecute trespassers were known, without affection, as wooden liars,

A community walk on the Malverns for a Methodists congregation in 1937. *(Russell Green)*

for trespass, a uniquely British law, was a civil, not a criminal, offence. A trespasser could not therefore be prosecuted in a criminal court, but only sued in a civil court. Under these circumstances the landowner would have to show that the trespasser had failed to leave his land when asked to do so and, in not doing so, had caused damage.

One of the leading lights in the Sunday Trampers was a lawyer, Sir Frederick Pollock. He helpfully devised a field defence against being sued for trespass. He advocated that, on being challenged, the hikers should, in unison, solemnly proclaim to the landowner or their agents that no 'claim of any right of way or other easement' was intended by their actions. In addition they should present the

Land Army girls on a country walk during the Second World War.
(Eve Lichfield)

surprised owner with a shilling piece 'by way of amends'.

For upper class men like those of the Sunday Trampers who, during the week, would patronise the same London clubs as the landowners themselves, countering a claim of trespass was something of an amusement. For the lower orders it was not. In the early 1900s the working class rambler was the new poacher. They could expect the same levels of violence that a keeper, armed with a cudgel or gun, normally reserved for the poacher. Spring guns, where a trip wire was attached to the trigger of a loaded gun aimed at the trespasser's legs, were still used: two members of the Sussex Pathfinders Ramblers' Club were injured by one as late as 1953. This was despite the Home Secretary Robert Peel's assertion that he could not approve the use of the spring gun in punishing a trespasser with death when the felon, if convicted, would normally face no more than a three month prison sentence. In the 1920s landowners in the Peak District were keen to exercise their own rights and took advertising space in the Manchester Evening Chronicle and to publish photographs of ramblers who had trespassed in the Peaks. The advertisements offered a £5 reward for the trespassers' names and addresses.

If matters did come to court, justice, as the old adage would have it, was as open to all as the Ritz Hotel. In 1892 a Sheffield saw-handle maker, Daniel Harrison, went to court after being roughed up by local gamekeepers as he walked a public footpath between Ringing Low and Hathersage in the Peak District. The keepers claimed that he had been trespassing and interfering with the rights of the owner, the Duke of Rutland, to exercise his sporting rights. The court found in Harrison's favour and awarded him damages of five shillings.

Three years later, in March, Stephen's Sunday Tramps held their 252nd and final ramble (although the Sunday Tramps club was reformed in the 1900s). But by now the formation of walking and hiking clubs was gaining momentum. Among the first was the Manchester YMCA Rambling Club, founded in 1880. A year later

KINDER SCOUT TRESPASSES

£5 REWARD

will be paid for the name, address and occupation
of any of the persons represented in the photos.

Apply:— CORBETT, WHEELER & CORBETT, Solicitors,
49, Spring Gardens, ——————— Manchester.

Ev.Chronicle   Monday Apl. 30 1923

Peak District landowners offered
£5 reward for information
on trespassers in the 1920s.
(Ramblers Association)

the Co-op Holidays Association with similar aims
to the Manchester Club was established. The Forest
Ramblers and Polytechnic Clubs opened in London
in 1884 and 1888, the Yorkshire Ramblers Club and
the Clarion Ramblers at Sheffield, led by G.H.B. Ward
in 1900. As the clubs proliferated, so were many
brought together as federations until in 1931 the
National Council of Ramblers' Federation, what was
to become the Ramblers' Association, was formed. The
first Federation, founded in London in March 1905
would be presided over by Sir Frederick Pollock who
had first found his walking feet with Leslie Stephen.

As Cyril Joad would put it, walking was becoming
better than beer for getting folk out of the city.

BENNY ROTHMAN
'The finest rambling country is closed to us'

The Peaks, the southern end of the Pennine Chain, is the wildly beautiful high land that looks down on industrial Manchester and Stockport in the west, and industrial Leeds and Sheffield in the east. At its centre lies the White Peak, its steep-sided flanks scored by stone walls and rolling fields, its subterranean galleries honeycombed with caves and caverns. Surrounding the White Peak is a horseshoe of millstone grit and moorland, the Black Peak, which rises up to the summits of Bleaklow and Kinder Scout, both over 2000 feet high. The seventeenth century poet Charles Cotton had already described the area as 'so deformed' they looked like 'Nature's pudenda'.

Ever since the opening of the Hope Valley railway line linking Manchester and Sheffield in 1894, hikers had been making their way up here, disembarking at Edale, Thornhill or Hathersage, before heading for the hills. The Peaks in the 1920s and 1930s attracted city hikers in their tens of thousands.

'The movement which has brought young towns-folk out on to the moors has hardly a parallel in Britain,' wrote Patrick Monkhouse in *One Foot in the Peak* (1932). Cyril Joad, a professor at the University of London and author *of The Untutored Townsman's Invasion of the* Country (1946) wrote that 'hiking has replaced beer as the shortest cut out of Manchester, as, turning their backs upon the cities which their fathers made, armies of young people make sorties . . . into the countryside.'

But there was a problem: those wooden liars. George Trevelyan spelled out the difficulties in his *Clio: A Muse and other Essays*. The Highlands, he said, had largely ceased to belong to Britain because of deer hunting. Now the grouse moors were going the same way. He blamed the grouse shooters who instructed their gamekeepers to close off the moor for 356 days a year. If the Alps were British, he suggested, they would long ago have been closed on account of the chamois.

What Joad called 'the curse of the keeper' had already closed off Kinder Scout, Bleaklow and the eastern moors of the Peak District. Guidebooks even warned about persistent trouble spots. Monkhouse pointed out to his readers that walkers on Sundays, crossing from South Head to Edale Cross on Kinder, should watch out for one particular keeper with his gun and dog. 'His presence is usually an adequate deterrent, and the gun has not yet been used.' These keepers who worked to rear, manage and stage the shooting of wild red grouse were posted to protect their masters' moors. Others were posted to keep ramblers out of the municipal water catchments.

So it was that on Sunday 24 April 1932 Manchester's London Road railway station resembled Wakes Week. The numbers streaming into the station matched the hundreds who, during the

Radical walker Benny Rothman revisits Kinder Scout. (Ramblers Association)

annual shutdown of the mills, packed their bags and departed for the coasts of Lancashire and north Wales. The summer holiday makers traditionally dressed in their Sunday best – the Blackpool land-ladies expected no less – but this April army wore shorts, open-necked shirts and studded boots that sparked on the cobbles. They were hikers. And they were headed for a mass trespass of Kinder Scout in the Peaks.

As landowners recruited extra men from the Peak villages to resist the trespass, a gaggle of policemen went to London Road railway station to rummage through the crowd. They were looking for a famil-iar face: Benny Rothman had been busy with his chalks.

The curse of the keepers closed off grouse moors to all but the shooting fraternity. (*Punch*)

Although he might more properly be described as the original, socialist walker, Benny Rothman was what the popular press would call a political agitator. He was born in 1911 and died in 2002 having devoted his life to the working class struggle. Brought up in working class Cheetham in north Manchester, Benny won a scholarship to Manchester Central High School, but had to quit school and work to support his widowed mother and family. He took up night school with the YMCA and he was soon in contact with communism. And the police. Having signed up with the Young Communist League in 1929 he was arrested the same year for chalking the challenging inscription 'Look out for the Daily Worker – out January 1st 1930' on a Manchester pavement. Magistrates saw fit to fine him 7s 6d. His employer made him redundant. It was no surprise that Benny spent the rest of his days as a militant trade unionist espousing causes as diverse as war-working women's pay, nuclear disarmament, the fight against a by-pass through the countryside of Twyford Down, and even a council plan to narrow a local footpath and so prevent mums walking down it with their prams.

Like many of his fellow workers Benny escaped the hardships of home by fell walking. His walking days almost came to an end during a fight with Oswald Mosley's Fascist Blackshirt brigade in 1933. At the Kings Hall in Manchester's Belle Vue, after stepping in to protect heckler Evelyn Taylor (later trades union leader Jack Jones' wife) from being beaten up, and chucking pro Fascist leaflets out of a balcony window, he was himself thrown from the balcony. Fortunately a Blackshirt below broke his fall.

Having climbed Snowdon, alone with his trusty 6d Woolworth's map given him on his sixteenth birthday, Benny was still walking in his eighties, often with his wife Lily, the Rochdale mill girl he met at peace camp. In the early 1930s, however, he combined his twin passions: hiking and political activism.

In 1931 Benny Rothman had helped found a local branch of the communist-backed British Workers' Sports Federation (BWSF) aimed at supporting and recruiting the young and often unemployed. Early in 1932, during a BWSF weekend camp in Howarth several young men and women from the camp were turned off the moors by the keepers. Angry and indignant they returned to camp and there hatched plans for a public trespass of Kinder Scout. Benny and his colleagues set to work with their chalks on the Manchester and Sheffield pavements, urging people to meet at Hayfield's Recreation Ground, below Kinder, on 24 April. Forewarned, the police moved in to pick up Benny at the London Road station. But their intelligence was flawed: Benny had bought a bike. A keen cyclist and member of the Clarion Cycling Club, Benny had chosen to by-pass the station by bike.

When Benny and the other demonstrators, variously estimated between 400 and 800, reached Hayfield Recreation Ground they found it ringed by police as the parish clerk read out a hasty injunction banning the meeting. The police rushed, and failed, to head them off, and the ramblers streamed up the valley towards Kinder reservoir and Kinder Scout, singing the Red Flag and International. They were accompanied by a reporter from the Manchester Guardian. 'As soon as we came to the top of the first steep bit we met the keepers,' he wrote. 'There followed a brief parley, after which a fight started. There were only eight keepers, while from first to last forty or more ramblers took part in the scuffle. The keepers had sticks, while the ramblers fought mainly with their hands, though two keepers were disarmed and their sticks turned against them.'

Keepers and ramblers clash on the Kinder Scout trespass. (Ramblers Association)

One keeper, from the Stockport Corporation Waterworks was knocked unconscious and carted off to Stockport Infirmary and then, the fighting over, the trespass continued to Ashop Head where a contingent from the Sheffield side, who had marched from Hope over Jacob's Ladder, joined the trespassers for tea. Carefully collecting up any litter the demonstrators walked back to Hayfield flushed with victory. When an amiable police inspector suggested they form an orderly column and march into the village behind his little car, they obliged. It was trap. As they entered Hayfield a snatch squad working with the keepers pulled Benny and others from the crowd. They were bustled away to a lock up at Hayfield, but moved back to New Mills after the efforts of fellow

The mass trespass to Kinder Scout on 24 April 1932. (Ramblers Association)

ramblers to break down the jail.

John Anderson, 21, of Droylsden, Bernard Rothman, 20, Julius Clyne, 23, Harry Mendel, 22, and David Nussbaum, 19, all of Cheetham, and Arthur Gillett, 19, a student at Manchester University, were charged with unlawful assembly and breaching the peace. Anderson was also charged with causing grievous bodily harm to the injured gamekeeper. At the trial in Derby Assizes in July, Rothman defended himself telling the court that, after a hard week's work, and life in a smoky city, rambling gave the working people a breath of fresh air and sunshine. Yet the finest country was closed to them by certain individuals who wished to shoot for about ten days a year.

The Judge, instructing jurors to ignore the foreign sounding names of several of the defendants (there were accusations of anti-semitism directed against the police), received the jury's mostly guilty verdicts. Rothman was given a four-month sentence, the others two, three, and in Anderson's case, six months. The grouse shooting season traditionally opens on the Glorious Twelfth, 12 August in the huntsman's calendar. That year the guns took up their positions on the moorland butts safe in the knowledge that Benny Rothman was behind bars, serving his sentence in Leicester jail.

Trevelyan thought it extraordinary that ordinary people should be prevented from enjoying the hills for the sake of killing a dozen more grouse a year. No landowner would agree: 'If these people were not engaged in fighting for access to mountains they would still find some other mischief for their idle fingers to do,' the Duke of Athol insisted in a letter to *The Field* in 1930.

Many BWSF members were bitter that the new National Council of Ramblers' Federation or the influential Manchester Ramblers Federation had failed to support their Kinder Trespass. Those organisations argued later that they had been in sensitive negotiations with the land-owning fraternity when the hot-headed young communards took matters into their own hands. Ironically the BWSF's trespass was associated in the public mind, especially by its more sedentary members, as being the work of the ramblers' movement as a whole. The idea that ramblers were dedicated not just to open access, but to the overthrow of the landed gentry was established then. The myth has persisted ever since.

Benny lived to regret it: the mass trespass, he wrote, was too important to be dismissed either as youthful folly, or as a political stunt. But he thought: 'We should never have antagonised the leaders of the Ramblers' Federation. We should perhaps have used our youthful zeal and energy inside the rambling movement.'

But the Kinder Trespass did make a very public point. Protest and pressure for public access continued to gain momentum. Even as Benny Rothman and his co defendants awaited their trial, a protest rally at Winnats Pass attracted thousands of ramblers. The walking world was about to change.

Footnote: The Devil's Rope

Liberally used to block footpaths and other rights of way, barbed wire was, according to W.H. Hudson, 'man's improvement on the bramble'.

Improved stock wire was patented nine times in America from 1868 to 1874, Michael Kelly registering the first 'thorny fence' with a double strand of wire fixed with barbs. Then Joseph Gilden, an Illinois farmer, patented his improved designs and a machine for its manufacture. The Winner brand or as the Native Americans called it, the Devil's Rope, carved up the Great Plains forever and deprived the cowboy of his livelihood. By 1888 it was being used by the British military and during the First

World War its manufacturers grew rich on its production. But in the post war years and ever since, a strand of barbed wire has come to symbolise the battle lines between land-owners and walkers.

TOM STEPHENSON
The Right to Roam – it's an old phrase
I've used over and over again

Every newspaper columnist has his moment of panic: the deadline looms, the weather is grey and all the author can think about is his mother's impending birthday. Tom Stephenson, open air correspondent for the *Daily Herald*, wrote a prodigious amount. Sometimes he struggled: 'For any wayfarer desiring an objective for his journey it is doubtful if there is a more fascinating subject than ancient highways and their associated features,' he wrote, straining to breathe new life into an old piece for the *Countryside Companion* in the 1930s. He had already written the introduction and nine of the previous chapters.

However he had no difficulties delivering the centre page spread for *The Herald* on 22 June 1935. Under the heading *Wanted – A Long Green Trail*, Stephenson revealed that two young women had written to him from the United States. America had just opened another long distance route, the John Muir Trail which wandered for 2,500 miles from the Canadian border through Washington, Oregon and California to Mexico. Having tackled that other classic hike the

Free to roam: a group of ramblers on a winter's walk in the Forest of Dean. (Arkitype)

Appalachian Way, a 2000 mile walk from Maine to Georgia, the women proposed a walking tour in Britain. Where, they wondered, were Britain's best long distance footpaths?

There were none. And, Stephenson mused: 'What will our visitors think of one of the most prevalent features in our landscape – "Trespassers Will Be Prosecuted"? Wherever they go, from Kent to Cornwall, from Sussex to the Solway Firth, they will see these wooden liars.' Nowhere, he added, was the situation worse than in Derbyshire's Peak District (although the Forest of Bowland and the Chatsworth and Saville Estates especially ran a close second).

Stephenson proposed his own long distance route, 'something akin to the Appalachian Way', over the Pennines from the Peak District to the Cheviot Hills

150 miles away. He traced out for his readers a route that could become a 'faint line on the Ordnance Maps which the feet of grateful pilgrims would, with the passing years, engrave on the face of the land'. His proposed path rose at Eadale, mounted the controversial Kinder Scout – still closed to all but grouse shooters and their keepers – follow Ashop Head, Bleaklow, over Saddleworth Moors to Stanedge and Blackstone Edge. Then, 'steering between the industrial blackspots' on to Boulsworth, past Pendle Hill over Fountains Fell and Pen-y-ghent to join the old packhorse trail into Wensleydale. From here the trail would touch Upper Swaledale, pass on over Stainmoor to the Pennines' highest point, Cross Fell, along the ancient Maiden Way, through the town of Alston, and over Hadrian's Wall to reach the 'swells and deep-set glens' of the Cheviots.

The new trail needed a name. Stephenson patriotically suggested the Georgian Path or the Jubilee Way since the reigning monarch, King George, was due to celebrate his Jubilee year. Twenty years later on 24 April 1965 Tom Stephenson stood on Malham Moor watching a drawn-out trail of hikers make their way along Britain's latest long distance footpath. It was called, not the Jubilee, but the Pennine Way.

Tom Stephenson, like Benny Rothman, was a self-educated man from a tough, working class background. Born in Chorley, Lancashire in 1893, Stephenson was the eldest of nine children whose father worked as an engraver at a calico printing works. His father was also the village clarinetist and

Tom Stephenson of the
Ramblers' Association beside
one of the infamous wooden
liars. (Ramblers Association)

a champion drinker. At the age of eight, Tom signed
the Abstinence Pledge at a Band of Hope meeting
on his father's behalf. His father did not give up the
bottle, but he did take the unusual step of keeping
the boy in school until he was thirteen. Too many
working class Lancashire children still worked the
half time system: half the time in school, half the
time down the mill.

When he reached thirteen Tom Stephenson
started as a labourer at a textile printing works.
He worked a twelve-hour shift, illegal even then,
starting at 6 a.m. Since there was no bus he walked
the two miles from his home in Whalley to the mill.
After work he walked another two miles to Clithero
library where he was studying. Then he walked the
four miles home. When he started studying at night

school in Burnley, eight miles from home, he took to cycling. He would cover around 6,000 miles over the next four years.

Stephenson walked to relieve the tyranny of work, like many working men, tramping up the Yorkshire Pennines to places such as Waddington Fell and Pendle Hill. On the first Saturday after he started work, he struck out for the hills. His home village of Whalley stood in the scenic Ribble Valley over-looked by Pendle Hill: Stephenson climbed its 560 metre summit and looked out over the Bowland Fells, Pen-y-ghent and the other Pennine peaks 'all snow covered . . . clear and sharp in the frosty air. That vision started me rambling and in the next 60 years took me time and again up and down the Pennines,' he wrote in *Forbidden Land* (1989). Usually walk-ing alone, and on little money, he expected to cover forty and even fifty miles in a day. He was still only fourteen when he made his first long distance hike through the Forest of Bowland and Cumbria, sleep-ing outdoors 'rolled in a groundsheet in the lee of a drystone wall' except for when one farming family took him in for the night. The grateful Stephens offered to pay: 'Thee keep it,' said the farmer's wife. 'Tha'll be wantin' it.'

In 1915 his studies paid off: he was awarded a scholarship to study geology at the Royal College of Science in London. 1916 saw Tom Stephenson in London, but not at the Royal College: he was in prison at Wormwood Scrubs for being a conscien-tious objector. 'The solitude of prison did not bother me so much as some people, because I had been accustomed to wandering day after day by myself over the hills,' he wrote in *Forbidden Land.* He was released from prison when the war finished, but, because of his prison record, refused his scholarship by the London College. Tom stayed in London, returned to his old craft of block printing, and joined the Labour Party. He also started to earn 'the occasional guinea' writing about rambling. It was this mix, rambling, writing and socialism, which would direct his career.

In 1926 he began editing *Hiker and Camper* magazine and working for the Trades Union Congress sponsored by *The Daily Herald.* Later he paid tribute to the paper's editors: 'They gave me a free hand. I'd write about Hills for the People, Guard your Footpaths and The Right to Roam, an old phrase of mine I have used over and over again down the years.' In 1934 he spoke to 3000 protestors at an access to moorlands demonstration at Winnats Pass, Castleton. In 1935 he penned his *Wanted – A Long Green Trail* for *The Herald.* Wherever and whenever he could, Stephenson lobbied for open access to mountains and moorlands. He was not the first. As far back as 1892, James Bryce, a president of the Alpine Club, proposed an access Bill declaring that 'land is not property for our unlimited and unqualified use.' There was, he said, 'no natural justice to such a thing as unlimited power of exclusion'. Neither this nor any subsequent attempt to improve public access to private moorlands and mountains could

A protest rally by ramblers at Winnats protesting against the sentences imposed on Rothman and his fellow walkers. (Ramblers Association)

dent the class act of land ownership. While no-one thought to question a citizen's right to freely wander the Swiss Alps, the Austrian Tyrol or the Spanish Pyrenees, much of Britain's moors and mountains remained closed to all but the few.

Finally in 1939 an Access to the Mountains Act made it onto the statute book. It was ironic that the Bill, which contained so many amendments and modifications that it represented no more than a protection bill for landowners, should be passed on the eve of a World War which would demand the ultimate sacrifice of over 330,000 people. But when that war had come and gone

Presenting his case for the Pennine Way, Tom Stephenson points out the route to Hugh Dalton with fellow walkers Barbara Castle, Fred Willey, Arthur Blenkinsop, George Chetwynd and Julian Snow. (Ramblers Association)

change was inevitable. It came quicker than might be expected, thanks to Tom Stephenson and an influential little hiking party.

Stephenson had become press officer for the Ministry of Town and Country Planning in 1943. It was 'a cheerless place permeated with a fear of publicity', but it gave him the opportunity to stalk Whitehall's corridors of power seeking converts to the cause of better access. He did not to trust the politicians. After the General Strike in 1926 one of his Parliamentary heroes, the Labour MP for Blackburn, Philip Snowden, had denounced an electioneering pamphlet in the House telling his fellow MPs that he had never seen the pamphlet before. Stephenson knew the Member for Blackburn had had a direct hand in its production. But Stephenson also knew that the access lobby needed to do business with the Honourable Members. He had known it when, as an eight year old and having failed to stop his father drinking, he had decided to become an MP and pass a law closing all pubs.

In 1948, with tramping rather than temperance in mind, Tom Stephenson proposed to a small group of MPs, sympathetic to his cause, that they should go rambling together. The hikers matched in influence, although not political allegiance, those who had trouped behind Leslie Stephen fifty years before. They included a former Chancellor of the Exchequer, Hugh Dalton, and the Labour MPs Barbara Castle, Fred Wiley, Arthur Blenkinsop, George Chetwynd and Julian Snow. 'He knew how to use politicians' admitted Barbara Castle to radio listeners in 1969.

In May 1948 he led them on their first hike across one of the finest sections of his proposed Georgian Way, from Teesdale over High Cup Nick, down to Dufton, across Cross Fell and up to Hadrian's Wall. Over the next few years Stephenson guided his group not through the by-ways of Stephens' Surrey, but through challenging, but beautiful territory: the Cheviots, the Lake District, the Pembrokeshire coast, the Brecon Beacons and the Peak District. It was no coinci-

Above the clouds!
very nice too – but
you must come down to
earth – sometimes

THE
RAMBLERS'
ASSOCIATION

Annual Subscription 5s

We've come a long way over the years...

A Ramblers
Assocation leaflet
with Stephenson's
wife Madge on Glydr
Fawr in Snowdonia.
(Ramblers
Association)

dence that each of the chosen routes ran though places where there was the possibility of creating one of the new, proposed National Parks. 'To see Tom sit down and put on his walking boots used to give me confidence,' recalled Barbara Castle. 'We politicians brought the panache, but Tom organised the route, guided us over the slippery slopes and got us there.' By now secretary of the Ramblers' Association, Stephenson was at the birth of the National Parks, still lobbying, campaigning and oiling the wheels of political power. His wife Madge (the couple had met after the First World War and stayed together for more than fifty

215

years until her death in 1982) was progressively disabled by arthritis and unable to join him on the fells. On one occasion, emerging from hospital after a minor operation she found, not Tom, but a neighbour waiting to take her home. 'If I were a national park Tom would be here,' she remarked without bitterness.

As chairman of the National Parks Commission's long-distance routes sub committee, Stephenson was directly involved in the designation of a succession of 'long green trails': Offa's Dyke, the Pembrokeshire Coastal Path, the South-West Peninsula Path, the North and South Downs Ways. Eventually the Pennine Way would be added to the list and, sixty years after he took over as secretary of the Ramblers Association, Britain boasted several hundred.

Tom Stephenson died in 1987, having seen the end of the kind of encounter he witnessed occurring on the summit of Great Whernside in Upper Wharfedale around 1929. Resting in the June sunshine on the summit, he noticed a keeper approached with his gun and dog.

'Dost tha' know tha' art trespassing?' the keeper asked.

'Aye, what are you going to do about it, prosecute or shoot?' Stephenson replied.

'Nay,' responded the keeper. 'Its aw reet as long as tha knows.'

STEPHEN GRAHAM
'You cannot tramp without boots'

While men like Rothman and Stephenson were campaigning for legal access, a contemporary of theirs, Stephen Graham, was tramping wherever he chose. Walking, thought Graham, was less about reaching the end of the journey than about satisfying one's curiosity. He proposed several methods of walking which made the most of their unpredictability.

A favourite was Trespasser's Walk which involved taking a compass, setting a straight course and then doggedly following it over ploughed fields and commons, graveyards and gardens, repairing broken hedges behind you, replacing fallen hurdles and averting your eyes if you happened upon a lady swimming in her private pool. The Trespasser's Walk was not as mad as it sounded: Graham spelled out the law of trespass, pointed out that while the odd 'peppery squire' might set his dogs on you or call the police, most of the people one encountered were usually pleased enough to meet a stranger and discuss their stock, the price of land or what that dreadful politician Ramsay MacDonald was up to. He advised against explaining the compass rule, – 'they will not take to it' – and to wear light clothing and shoes since you would often have to jump.

His random walking methods aside, Stephen Graham was one of the most remarkable walkers of the first half of the twentieth century and one who provided his readers with all they needed to know

A tiny reproduction of a Russian peasant with a dead bear, photographed by Graham in Russia. (Vologda Oblast Government)

about hiking, from what to carry in their rucksacks, to the practicalities of taking a hiking honeymoon. (A tramping honeymoon, he thought, was the ideal way to begin married life.)

Graham was born in the 1880s. Having started work in London he spontaneously quit his job after reading the work of the Russian Maxim Gorky.

The walker's friend,
an early Silva compass
produced in 1932
and ideal for one of
Stephen Graham's
'Tresspasser's Walks'.
(Silva Sweden AB)

Whatever it was about Gorky that so inspired him, Graham picked up his walking boots – 'you cannot tramp without boots' – and went wandering through Russia and Siberia. He walked in the Middle East, in America and in Central Asia. The 1914-18 War interrupted his 6,000-mile journey from southwest Russia to the northwest, but in 1915 Graham was walking through Egypt, Bulgaria and Romania; a year later it was Norway and Murmansk. He joined the Scots Guards towards the end of the War and found himself on foot again, this time marching through a defeated Germany.

Each walk produced a book, each book prompted another walk and Graham continued writing and walking from 1912 until 1956.

In 1921 he walked for six weeks through the Glacier Park in British Columbia with the poet Vachel Lindsay, 'an old fashioned hiker of the tramping person type'. Like Thoreau before him and Gary Snyder after, Lindsay had a powerful affection for hiking. He had taken to the American trails of the eastern highlands and the South in 1909 at the age of 30, trading, as he put it, 'rhymes for bread'. His contact with the everyday people gave his poetry the voice of Middle America and, for a while, he received much admiration for works such as *In Praise of Johnny Appleseed*. He and Graham, who wrote that there was no greater test of friendship than taking a long tramp together, made good walking companions. After his initial celebrity status, however, Lindsay's fortunes declined. Ten years after their walk, he took his own life.

Graham continued to walk, to south America to glimpse for himself Cortez's view of the Pacific; to Russia where the new administration refused him entry – Graham turned back and walked around the country from Lake Logoda to the Black Sea; and through Dalmatia, the Balkans and, in 1925, the Caspathians.

By now, Graham was well placed to advise on the best places to walk. Britain, although unsuitable for sleeping under the stars, nevertheless offered some adventurous tramps in the West Country, Cumberland and the Highlands. He recommended the Welsh Marches too, especially Shropshire. While Wales itself could be wild, the walker should carry a couple of day's provisions because of the difficulty of making oneself understood in English. Donegal and Dartmoor both met with his approval, while

America and Canada represented a tramper's paradise. France was fine for an inn to inn pilgrimage especially if the walker substituted a litre bottle for the coffee pot and filled it with the regional *vins du pays*. The beauty of the Basque country around the Pyrenees was as wild and delightful as traversing the Provençal hills to Cannes. The walker in Spain could anticipate tramping through untouched countryside although walkers should expect to be regularly stopped by the police. (There were two sure ways to avoid trouble: never wear tweeds and always carry a guitar).

Northern Italy was cheap, Austria roomy, Southern Germany expensive and Bavaria: well, Bavaria was Bavaria and fine if you enjoyed the beer. Switzerland, as a breeding ground for lounge lizards and lazy tourists had its drawbacks, but 'Czecho-Slovakia' and the Balkan states, Dalmatia, Montenegro and Albania, offered plenty of wild walking, Albania especially where walking should be undertaken only with an armed guard.

Graham returned to England each winter to write up his previous journey, but in 1925 he stayed behind in a little Dalmatian village and later in Ragusa, which he called Europe's most beautiful city, in order to pen the definitive walker's guide, *The Gentle Art of Tramping*. 'Know how to tramp and you know how to live,' promised Graham as he provided a wealth of good advice.

For footwear he recommended a new pair of army boots. He confessed, however, that he had never been able to improve upon a pair of 'chrome leather' fishing boots, bought at a roadside store in the Catshill mountains. His feet had been suffering from blisters by day and frost by night; now, he was able to walk painlessly to Chicago in his new boots.

The sensible tramper would wear two or three pairs of socks and flush their feet daily in a mountain stream or, better still, the sea, and eschew road walking for mountain trails. The mountains, he explained, not only offered more distraction, but also, as one's feet fell upon uneven ground, employed more muscles. He had observed his friend Vachel Lindsay experiencing problems with 'bradded boots' – they could slip on rocks – and offered a testimonial to Phillips' rubbers fitted to light boots for such excursions. In fact if the tramper wished to be totally equipped they should carry a pair of light tennis shoes for rock scrambling. The addition of tennis shoes and, to be absolutely prepared, a duplicate pair of boots raised the question of what should go into the average tramper's rucksack.

Graham insisted upon the following: a blanket (or two; or at least a pair of double sheets sewn on three sides to form a sleeping bag); a waterproof cape or oilskin; soap, towel and comb; a change of clothes, plenty of handkerchiefs, a housemaid's 'tidy' and a collar and tie (for the purpose of visiting post offices, banks, a priest or the police); a few yards of mosquito net; notebook, or diary, fountain pens and ink and a volume of poems printed with broad margins for annotation purposes; knife, spoon, enamel mug,

First class footwear was essential for the seasoned walker, insisted Stephen Graham.

plate (a fork was unnecessary); pepper and salt, mixed to taste; food, a safe box for butter, coffee and a plain metal cafetière hung outside the rucksack from the centre strap. Oh, and a glove for lifting the said pot off the fire. An air pillow was 'not to be despised', while a revolver was best left at home. In wild places such as the Caucasus, the weapon itself was likely to become the cause of a robbery.

As for the rucksack only one made in Germany or Austria would do: he had purchased his favourite from a shop in Vienna after twelve hours of negotiations: the shopkeeper had insisted the item was not for sale. Exterior pockets, which did not burst, were useful; interior pockets too to avoid the intermingling of coffee grains and linen. Alternatively the tramper could place items in cheap cotton bags, purchasable from Woolworth's and tied with tapes. Graham was a practical man.

As for a dress code Graham suggested a khaki blouse, knickers (as in Dutch style knicker bockers) green puttees or stockings and a stout pair of shoes for women. For the man a collarless shirt (top button preferably undone) workman's trousers held up by braces (Graham specifies those marked for policeman and firemen), a jacket and a tweed hat with a brim. He warned that once you slept a night in your hat it became a hat for life, although no longer suitable for 'town wear'.

Thus equipped and dressed, he argued, the tramper could set out, liberated from his daily grind, from being a voter, a taxpayer, a grade three clerk ('or a grade two clerk who has reached his limit'). Graham railed against the class divisions that so divided the British nation, ('the most disgusting institution of civilisation because it puts a barrier between man and man'), and pointed out that a tramper could be anyone, pilgrim, explorer or Bohemian, except any of those 'won't works', and parasites on society such as hobos or beachcombers. His sentiments contrast with those of his contemporary, Canon Cooper who was more sympathetic towards the impoverished tramp.

As to money, a walker who slept out should manage on a shilling a day except in America where the tramper would need three quarters of a dollar. A large currency note for emergencies should be sewn into the jacket lining and not left in any secret pocket: he had done so once with a £5 note and panicked after handing the shirt to a peasant girl to launder. The honest lass found and removed the note, washed the shirt and returned both to him.

We cannot leave Stephen Graham without reviewing his second favourite form of walking, the Zigzag Walk, which he had usefully employed in London, Paris and New York. The Zigzag Walk involved taking the first turning on the left and the next on the right and seeing where it led. The Zigzag Walk was especially profitable in such cities as Paris, New York and London. A Christmas zigzag walk with his wife started somewhere around Curzon Street, lead them through Pulteney market, Covent Garden, Rupert Street and Callard's cake shop in Regent's Street. After mustard and cress sandwiches at Callard's they paused at Louis Gautier's in Swallow Street, plunged into Piccadilly, popped in to Hatchards and walked on by way of Duke Street, Jermyn Street and other 'asphalt alleys' to St James Place and Green Park and St James Park.

Their random central London tour continued by Buckingham Gate, Wilfred Street, Palace Street and concluded finally at Victoria 'where we took an omnibus home'.

HERBERT GATLIFF

'Bishop and blacksmith shall be equally welcome,
provided . . . they share the washing-up'

Technology revolutionised the business of sleeping
outdoors. By the turn of the millennium, plastics had
given the hiker a lightweight means of surviving the
dark hours in relative comfort. But it was only relative.
The average rucksack packed for a three-day tramp
might contain tent, poles, pegs, sleeping bag, self-
inflating mat, stove, fuel, dehydrated food, clothes,
waterproofs, gaiters, washbag, micro-towel, maps,
head torch, folding cutlery, cooking pans, knife,
vacuum food flask, polycarbonate plate set, digital
camera . . .

Thus is the walker confronted with that same
dilemma faced by every long distance walker since
Coryate set out from his Somerset village: how to
travel light yet still spend the night in some comfort. A contemporary of Tom Stephenson, Herbert
Gatliff, believed there was one sensible solution:
the hostel. Indeed the walking Whitehall civil servant was so committed to hostelling that he established his own chain of hostels on what he called
Europe's outer edge, the Outer Hebrides.

A clergyman's son, Herbert Gatliff was born
in 1897 at Alveley, Shropshire and buried in the
family grave at Breinton in Herefordshire eighty
years later having served as a soldier (briefly, for
six months in the First World War), a civil servant
and a charity worker. At Rugby School he became

Character building. The young Herbert Gatliff joined the Southern Pathfinders later the Croydan YHA club. (Elizabeth Gatliff)

a classics scholar under the influence of his classics master, the Rev'd H. H. Symonds, a committed outdoor enthusiast. Symonds campaigned as strongly in favour of National Parks and the protection of the Lake District as he did against the Forestry Commission's forestation of places such as Ennerdale in west Cumbria. Gatliff went up to Baliol College, Oxford along with a future prime minister, Harold Macmillan.

In the 1930s he joined a walking club, the Southern Pathfinders (later the Croydon YHA Group). Gatliff was firmly convinced that walking in the fresh air was character building stuff. As he wrote in the Pathfinders' club news: 'From being much in the country and the open air we grow harder and tougher; we learn to lead a keener, simpler life than that of the town, to find our own way to go without things, to endure fatigue and sometimes a certain amount of hardship.'

Before the youth hostel movement gained pace

he was not averse to spending the night under canvass although he preferred 'a camp bed with a comfortable spring mattress'. He could agree with V.G. Billier who extolled the virtues of camping in *The Countryside Companion*. Camping, he asserted, helped a man to become a good citizen, 'and the health-giving powers of recreation in the open air are widely recognized as being of great assistance in the creation of an A1 nation.'

Billier was full of useful advice for the camper. For the solo camper he recommended the 5 lb (2.25 kg) Midge, winner of the 1934 Camping Club Award of Merit, which was simple to erect, very stable in high winds and a speedy drier in the rain thanks to its steep pitch. Not that rain would worry the average camper: 'If it does rain (the camper) comforts himself with the fact that it does not rain forever. Besides . . . is there not some consolation in listening to the beating of the rain on the tent walls and in the sweet smell of the grass after rain has fallen?' For many there was not.

The answer in the early 1930s was a hostel bed. The Youth Hostel Association (YHA) had been founded in 1931 and it was fired with enthusiasm for providing plain lodgings – a bed for a shilling a night for walkers. (The 'Youth' in Youth Hostel, explained the Ramblers Association's Tom Stephenson, was measured in spirit, not in years.) The Youth Hostel movement had been started

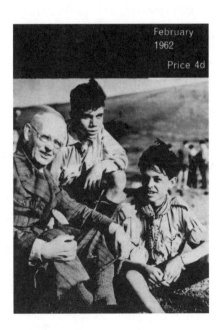

Richard Schirrman, German schoolmaster and founder of the youth hostelling movement. (YHA)

in Germany in 1910 by a schoolmaster Richard Schirrman. It aimed to help all (but especially 'young people of limited means') to 'a greater knowledge, love and care of the countryside, by providing hostels or other simple accommodation for them in their travels.' (The wit offered an alternative description of youth hostelling as going camping with a more or less fixed roof.) The early hostels were to be set up along the classic hiking routes such as the Pilgrims' Way. But as George Macaulay Trevelyan, president of the YHA and author of *Clio, a Muse* reported in the first issue of *Rucksack* magazine in 1931: 'Now we are breakfasted, booted and on the march, and by all accounts we are catering for the young men and women we set out to serve . . . folk who take their holidays strenuously and joyously.'

Gatliff enjoyed the chummy, communal atmosphere of hostel life. 'I think the chief event of the Club's last year has been our discovery of Youth Hostels,' he declared in the Pathfinder's newsletter. The names, he wrote, were full of romance – Derwent Hall, Black Sail, Shottery, Maeshafn, Brendon and Dartmeet sounding like a peal of church bells calling out to the rambler.

He had his favourites such as the City Mill at Winchester, a converted mill on the River Itchen where hostellers could descend into the bowels of the building to bathe, clinging to a rope, in the mill stream. The rope was essential: 'Legend has it that someone was once swept out of his bath into

A group of ramblers outside Idwal Cottage Hostel, opened in Snowdon in 1931. For Gatliff the chummy atmosphere of hostel life was perfect. (YHA)

the open stream, to the distress of the good people of Winchester.' The City Mill was a busy hostel and the busier the hostel, the more regimented the life within – 'lights out is no empty command at Winchester,' Gatliff warned.

Another thriving hostel was Lepham's Bridge in the Ashdown Forest. The forty-six year old Gatliff described a night out at Lepham's after a twenty-five mile tramp on a sweltering August Bank Holiday in 1933. Arriving hot and bothered he and his companions had hoped to find a lake in which to bathe (Gatliff was inclined to take a swim in the buff whenever the opportunity arose). Instead

As a civil servant
Herbert Gatliff
would travel to
work in Whitehall
with his trusty
rucksack.
(Elizabeth Gatliff)

they were greeted by a twilight scene of hostellers crowded on every available bench, eating cold suppers of tomatoes, egg and cheese, and drinking tea by the glimmer of oil lamps. The warden was handing out blankets for the night. After supper the weary walkers sang songs while the warden's wife played. 'We sang fitfully and not very tunefully maybe, but with our hearts full of the afterglow of sunset. Some of the old songs, one above all, Annie Laurie, I shall never forget; it was one of those rare moments when time stands still.'

Herbert Gatliff was, by now, a high ranking civil

servant in the Treasury. He was also one of those curious characters sometimes found among the sons and daughters of the clergy: passionate about minority rights, unmoved by the company of either lords or labourers, and quite clearly eccentric. In London, taking the Northern Line tube train to Whitehall from his Hampstead Gardens home, he habitually wore his Homburg hat (and occasionally his shorts) and carried his umbrella and rucksack. He kept his trusty primus stove and hiking boots in an office cupboard so that he might go hostelling straight from work – without his wife. He once complained that when she joined him at a hostel in Cornwall (she had put up at a nearby hotel) her presence had destroyed the atmosphere.

He was an inveterate letter writer, famed (and sometimes dreaded) for his missives written in small, triplicate copy books bought from Woolworth's, and slipped into envelopes marked 'URGENT'. Unfortunately his handwriting was, although not illegible, so nearly so that the recipient was obliged to spend hours deciphering it. The replies, when they arrived, were filed in the ranks of Cornflake packets Gatliff kept at home for the purpose. The number of cereal boxes devoted to the Outer Hebrides proliferated from the 1950s when Gatliff retired from the civil service and started his annual pilgrimage to the western isles. A journalist on the *Stornoway Gazette and West Coast Advertiser*, James Shaw Grant, described meeting him (*Herbert Gatliff: An English Eccentric*). 'I was told by one of

A Gaitliff hostel on Berneray in the Outer Hebrides housed in the traditional *tigh dubh* or blackhouse

the staff there was a tramp at the door who wanted to speak to me.' The long-haired, weather-beaten man who strode into his office wore a dilapidated, wartime, camouflaged gas cape: it was Herbert Gatliff, a little the worse for wear after weeks of walking the islands.

The industrialist and former chairman of the YHA, John Cadbury, had introduced Gatliff to the sternly beautiful Outer Hebrides or Western Isles. From Catholic Barra in the south to Protestant Lewis in the north, the necklace of crofters' islands that sheltered the Isle of Skye, were virtually tree-free. The white sand of the empty beaches spilled into the sea and the macha, stretches of shell sand and grassland, were filled with wild birds. The islands were dotted with the ruined remains of tigh dubh, the blackhouses, many of them sad memorials to the notorious Highland clearances of the 1800s, which saw landowners evicting tenants to release land for the more lucrative sheep farming. The only thing missing, in Gatliff's eyes, were hostels and he devoted the rest of his life (and much of his money) to founding the chain of Gatliff hostels, most housed in the restored or rebuilt *tigh dubh*.

A handful of people stayed in the first, Rhenigdale, when it was opened on North Harris in 1962. In 2005 over 1000 people, mostly young, but from every conceivable background, stayed there. As Gatliff put it: 'Bishop and blacksmith shall be equally welcome, provided . . . they share the washing-up'.

CHAPTER 6

ROUTE-MASTERS AND
RECORD BREAKERS

HUGH MUNRO AND WILLIAM POUCHER
Men 'who loved wild places'

Sir Hugh Thomas Munro, did not travel light when
he walked the Scottish hills. In the closing years of
the nineteenth century, Munro, the celestial sounds
of the hills singing gently in his ears, added compass, aneroid barometer, thermometer and measur-
ing poles to his overnight pack as he set off into the
night.

A soldier, mountaineer and Scottish laird, Munro
was born into a background of wealth and privilege
in 1856. He enjoyed the usual interests of his gen-

eration such as blood sports and Highland games, but he also found himself drawn to some of the less orthodox. He was intrigued by the art of dowsing and was convinced of the existence of heavenly music in the hills. (Perhaps there was such a phenomenon: Edward Elgar once told a friend that if he should ever hear a snatch of music while walking the Malvern Hills after the composer's death, it would probably be his.) He was also fascinated by mountains. He had taken up climbing during a holiday in the Alps in 1873. Now from his ancestral seat in Angus and with the Grampian Mountains to the northwest and the Cairngorms behind, Munro mused about the accurate definition of a mountain. A useful benchmark, since so few summits were above and so many below, was 3,000 feet (despised by A. Wainwright as 914.63m) which was why, in 1889, the Scottish Mountaineering Club asked the laird to produce an accurate list of all Scottish summits of 3,000 feet and above.

Munro took longer than expected over his list, not least because, although he was a paid up member of the shooting class, there were those among the Scottish aristocracy who regarded their mountains as out of bounds to anyone but themselves. The bearded and wiry Munro simply scaled and measured them by night, and in winter.

By 1891 the Scottish Mountaineering Club was able to publish the Munro tables, listing precisely 283 peaks. Almost immediately there was dissension over the Munro list: a hill that rose to a neat pinnacle

The Scottish Mountaineering Club defined a mountain as a peak over 3,000 feet. Hugh Munro set out to count them. (Arkitype)

3,000 feet high could clearly be classed as a Munro, but in a confusion of neighbouring peaks which, exactly, was the mountain? There were suggestions that Munro had selected summits more on the basis of their landscape qualities than the readings on the aneroid barometer.

Munro was appointed president of the Club in 1894 and, while he had surveyed 283 peaks, he had yet to walk them all. He set out to do so, but in 1919 he was struck down by pneumonia at a field hospital in southern France. He died before he could bag his final three Munros. In 2005 with the official Munro count at 284 a West Yorkshire steel worker, Steve Perry, set out to walk them all in one continuous journey. It was not the first time the 1500 miles journey had been undertaken. Perry, however, chose to walk them in midwinter and within 120 days. He started on 1 December 2005 climbing Ben More on The Isle of Mull and finished on the summit of Ben Hope in Sutherland precisely 120 days later.

While Munro, the walking laird, lay on his death-bed in France in 1919, Captain William Poucher, Walter to his friends, was being demobbed. Having joined the War as a twenty-three year old civilian dispenser of pharmaceuticals, he eventually served in France with the 41st Casualty Clearing Station. He was lucky to have survived, but then Walter Poucher, with two careers ahead of him, was lucky in life. He was also a man with some unlikely passions. There was nothing unusual about his partiality for golf or fast cars (he was especially fond of his pre-World War Two Jaguar). But he was also an accomplished pianist with an enthusiasm for Chopin, a high class perfumer, a first class landscape photographer, a mountaineer and a walker.

Poucher was born at Horncastle in Lincolnshire and, after the First War, worked in the soap making and perfume industry, becoming chief perfumer with the cosmetics firm, Yardley. He created their prestigious Bond Street perfume and stayed with the company until he retired in 1960. His colleagues presented him with a new Leica camera, appropriately enough since the sixty nine year old had already embarked on a second successful career as landscape photographer and routemaster.

Walter Poucher, may not have scaled all the

Routemaster
Walter Poucher,
the grand man of
the mountains.
(John Pucher)

Munros, but he photographed many of them and
went on to cover the Welsh, Lakeland and Pennine
peaks as well as the hills of Surrey, Ireland, the West
Country and the Dolomites. (John Hillaby in *Journey
Home* described him as a photographer whose profile
resembled the south face of Great Gable in the Lakes.)
He published four classic guides with routes over

the Lake District, Wales, Scotland and the Pennines, adding these to works on cosmetics and soaps, including *Eve's Beauty Secrets*. First published in 1926 it was still in print eighty years later.

Poucher's classic guides sold over 300,000 and still guides fell walkers around the summits of the Lakes, Wales, Scotland and the Pennines. John Hillaby, who often consulted him in his researches, called him that 'Grand Old Man of the Mountains'. Those who stop to admire the view of Skye from the bench outside the Sligachan Hotel might note the small brass plaque: 'Walter Poucher 1891 − 1988. A renowned mountain photographer who loved the wild places.'

'A.WALKER'
'Everything was wonderful. Even the rain'

In 1952 the Americans had exploded a hydrogen bomb, John Cobb had been killed attempting the water speed record on Loch Ness and the English artist Henry Moore had unveiled his leviathan modern sculpture, King and Queen. But the Borough Treasurer in the Town Hall at Kendal in Cumbria was bored. Forty five and putting on weight, he had recently finished building his new house and embarked on a five year plan to landscape the garden into a miniature version of the Lake District. The task, complete with tiny hills, cairns and boulder-laden crags, had taken only two years. He was at a loss over what to do next.

Not that he lacked an interest. Away from his desk

at the Town Hall the Borough Treasurer spent every hour of the day, and many of the night, fell walking. His flat cap clamped to his head, his pipe clamped between his teeth and a local map in his pocket, he stomped the hills and dales of the Lake District alone. "I always consider myself, when alone, a vastly entertaining companion but when with others am considered unsociable, boorish, not with it," he would write in his biography, *Memoirs of a Fellwalker*.

He emerged from his ennui by turning to what he described as his favourite literature – maps. He embarked on a series of hand-written walking guides to the Lakes, each illustrated with his own, detailed hand drawings. He was a pen and ink man, totally opposed to machinery (computer technology would eventually drive him from office. He was delighted to go.) He had, he said, no wish to romanticize the hills, but simply to draw them as they were. He even described his drawings as fraudulent since he photographed the fells by day and then, with the photographs as *aide memoirs*, revisited them at night on the drawing board. By 1965 he had published seven pictorial guides, each with his trademark signature, A. Wainwright.

A.W. tried to keep his Christian name secret, but the guides sold well and he became a reluctant celebrity. On the hills this reluctance verged on the ill-tempered. Encountering a party of walkers he would concede a gruff mumble to the first in line and ignore the echoing hellos of the rest of the party, leaving them to conclude that he was an unsociable grump

The young 'A.Walker' alias Alfred
Wainwright. (Courtesy of the
estate of A. Wainwright)

(which, of course, he was). If pressed, especially by an
attractive lady, he might own up to being the famous
A.W. but generally he denied it, giving his name, pun-
ningly, as A. Walker.

A.W. took to mounting the fells in the evening to
avoid such encounters. He would wait for first light,
keeping warm by pacing to and fro in the dark. For
a while he took an army blanket, but soon gave it
up because he was always too excited to sleep. Like
William Hutton he spent the dark hours reliving his
life, and trying to recall the women who might have
married him had he asked. (This passed the time, not
because there were so many of them, but because
he had so many doubts over the few.) Finally, as first
light broke and the rising sun burned off the mists,
Wainwright could continue his detailed documenting

The Blackburn Town Hall Walking Club with a youthful Alfred Wainwright, pipe in hand, on the left. (Courtesy of the estate of A. Wainwright)

of the Lakes without being distracted by other walkers.

There was no secret to Wainwright's Christian name. Born in a working class district of Blackburn, Lancashire in 1907, he had been christened Alfred. He was a clever lad, but family circumstances (his father, a stonemason, was more inclined to spend his wages on drink than housekeeping) pointed him towards a future as one of Blackburn's cotton mill workers. When drizzle forced the children off the streets at night, Wainwright sat under the gaslight writing and illustrating his own stories. Someone gave him a map of Lancashire, and Wainwright not only spent hours producing a replica of the map – his copying skills were legendary and his elementary school walls were decorated with his work – he also spent days walking its routes.

When he reached twelve his teachers persuaded his parents to send him to the higher elementary school. The working class boy fretted about matching the academic pace of his more affluent classmates. He need not have worried. He came top of his class in all but chemistry and physics, two subjects that, he said, he never understood. But a working family in the 1920s could not afford to keep even a bright breadwinner at home and a year later Wainwright left school to become a white-collar worker in the town's borough engineering department. Wainwright's childhood came to an end with his first pay packet of fifteen shillings, his first pair of long trousers and his first pair of glasses.

Wainwright remained a council worker for the rest of his working life. He took, and breezed through, his accountancy exams after studying at night school and, in 1941, moved to the treasurer's office in Kendal, eventually becoming Borough Treasurer. In the meantime he pursued any avenue that took him away from a loveless first marriage to a local mill girl. He founded a Blackburn Rovers football supporters club, became local organiser for the wartime Holidays At Home scheme, and walked the hills.

He began fell walking in 1930 when tramping the hills was one of the most popular pastimes for working men and women. He and his cousin Eric Beardsall took the bus from Bradford over the Pennines to the Lake District, sixty miles away. On their first hike, the pair climbed up through sunny-dappled village lanes on to the bare headland of Orrest Head.

While his cousin dozed, Wainwright looked from the summit across the mountains and lakes, over the crystal rivers and winding tracks that crisscrossed the heather. It was a Wordsworthian moment, a spot of time, that 'changed my life: its hauntingly perfection gave me no rest afterwards,' he wrote in *Fellwanderer,* the story behind the Guidebooks.

Wainwright's no nonsense writing style had a wry charm. *Fellwanderer* was aimed at those familiar with his guidebooks. It would, he said bluntly, interest few others because he had no thrilling adventures to recount. But the Fells brought him, and the thousands who trod in his footsteps, peace and placidity. Not that Wainwright was ever shy about expressing his opinions. Football hooliganism, for example, could be cured overnight if the authorities introduced the penalty of castration. He advocated similar punishments for anyone found guilty of ill treating animals.

He was especially furious about metrication when it was introduced to Britain and refused to quote altitudes in anything but British feet even in 1988 when he completed *Wainwright In Scotland.* To do so otherwise would give unwarranted satisfaction to the Brussels pen-pushers and insult the noble Scottish Highlands. Scotland was second only to the Lake District in Wainwright's affections: indeed he always holidayed north of the Scottish borders. His first visit to Scotland, to climb the mountains of Arran, was on the eve of the Second World War in 1939. He never forgot the moment of his departure when a group of villagers spontaneously broke into the song *Will ye no' come back again?* as he stepped on to the ferry at Brodick. He did return, time and again.

One particular walk in 1950 serves to illustrate the mindset of a determined walker. He had arrived at Ullapool on the MacBrayne's bus in mid afternoon and, rather than wait till morning, set off for Lochinver. He knew the local hotel, ten miles distant, had been closed after a fire, but hoped to find a bed and breakfast on the way. He failed and instead spent the night sheltering in the burned-out wreck of the hotel. At daybreak he struggled on, by now hungry, dehydrated and hallucinating a welcoming row of cottages in the distance. He was, as he put it 'absolutely buggered' when he eventually reached sanctuary, a bed and breakfast five miles from Lochinver. The landlady was so concerned for him that she walked to Lochinver and back to buy fresh fish for his supper. Such acts of generosity endeared Wainwright to the Scots. He declared them to be his favourite people.

Aside from documenting the hills of the Lake District and Scotland, Wainwright also devised the Coast to Coast walk. In 1973, having spent nights poring over his maps, Wainwright created a walk that wove through three National Parks from St Bees in western Cumbria to Robin Hood's Bay on the east coast. (Wainright recommended that walkers bathed their feet in both the Irish and the North seas). Although his 192 mile route travelled roads that, thirty years later, were too dangerous to walk

Although Wainright preferred his own company on the hills, he inspired a generation of new walkers such as these setting out at for a walk in Dovedale. (YHA)

because of the traffic, and which trespassed over private ground, the thirteen day hike has been described as one of the world's favourite long distance walks, second only to the Milford Trail in New Zealand. In 2007 his supporters were still campaigning for an official Coast to Coast route.

Alfred Wainwright died in 1991. He had produced over forty guides and volumes of drawings from the Lakes and Scotland. He may have regretted popularising the very places that he preferred to walk in solitude, but he made the most of the book royalties, pouring them not into the family purse, but an animal welfare charity, the Wainwright Shelter.

His devoted second wife, Betty, carried out his final wish: to have his ashes scattered by the side of the Innominate Tarn on Haystacks where the lake lapped the shore beneath the Pillar and Gable. In a typical aside to readers of *Fellwanderer* he concluded: 'If you, dear reader, should get a bit of grit in your boot as you are crossing Haystacks in the years to come, please treat it with respect. It might be me.'

FRANK NOBLE
'This National path is a farce'

Every year they appear like spring migrants, bobbing along the ridgeways and valleys that separate the Welsh hills from the English planes. In the sixties they were, with their anoraks and bobble hats, a hardy few. Now robed in Gore Tex and armed with lightweight walking poles, they stride out to tackle one of the more relaxed of the UK's burgeoning long distance footpaths (although it is said to have more knee-breaking stiles – 678 – than any other). They are the Dykers, walkers who will spend anything from ten days to three weeks tramping for 177 miles (283 km) along the longest archaeological monument in Britain, Offa's Dyke. It was all thanks to a Mercian king and a Yorkshire schoolmaster.

King Offa, who ruled the English Midland kingdom of Mercia from 757 to 796 (and during whose reign the penny piece was introduced), almost certainly commissioned the dyke that bears his name and almost certainly did so to keep out the warring Welsh. Offa's predecessor, King Aethelbert had been defeated by the Welsh in 722 and there were great

The arrival of spring and another group of walkers along the Offa's Dyke Path. (Arkitype)

battles between the Welsh and the Mercians at the border city of Hereford in 760, 778 and 784. Offa's Dyke was built to divide and rule. It was no low-key border crossing. A defensive earthwork up to twenty metres wide was built up to a height of eight metres high along a ditch which, mostly, faced Wales. It may have been topped with a timber palisade and gangs of labourers devoted at least four million man hours to its construction. Offa died in 796, possibly before his Dyke was completed.

There are many 'possibilities' concerning the story of the Dyke. There was, for example, a gap in the Dyke where it should have run across the good red earth of the Herefordshire plain. This may have been

Frank Noble getting to grips with that 'farce of a path' Offa's Dyke. (Jean O'Donnell)

due to the presence of an impregnable boggy oak wood, a kind of Tolkeinesque Fargon forest, which kept both sides at bay. Yet, where the lie of the borderland presented plenty of natural defensive positions, as above the Wye at Tintern, the workers still laboured over their dyke – or were these the vestiges of a different dyke altogether?

Not surprisingly the secret histories that lay buried beneath the eight-hundred-year-old track way caught the imagination of many antiquaries. Thomas Pennant, who referred to it as Offa's ditch, led readers of his *Tours In Wales* along the route in 1778. The ditch 'extended from the river Wye along the counties of *Hereford and Radnor* in to that of

Montgomery, where I fhall take it up at its entrance into North Wales at *Pwll y Piod*, an ale houfe on the road between Bifhop's-caffle and *Newton*.'

Pennant thought the ditch must run from 'fea to fea'. Bishop John Asser had already said so in his Life of Alfred in 893: 'The formidable King Offa . . . ordered the great rampart to be built between the Welsh and Mercia from sea to sea', he wrote. Pennant also thought the ditch had been constructed to contain the Welsh, but declared it inadequate to its task. 'The weakness of this great work appeared on the death of Offa', he wrote. 'The Welfh, with irrefiftible fury, defpifed his toils, and carried other ravages far and wide in the English Marches.' This, he explained, led King Harold to decree that any Welshman found on the Saxon side of the ditch should 'lofe his right-hand.'

Another historian drawn to the Dyke (and another convinced that the Dyke ran from sea to sea) was Sir Cyril Fox who, having arranged for several excavations along the ditch, publishing his own findings. Then, in 1950, an enthusiastic walker and historian from Yorkshire, Frank Noble, took up a teaching post at a secondary school in the sleepy mid Wales town of Knighton. Knighton, or *Tref-y-clawdd* as its Welsh name explained, was the town that straddled the dyke. The twenty-three year old Noble was drawn to the mysteries and the magnitude of this local landmark.

In 1955 Offa's Dyke was one of six routes to be designated as a long distance path. Yet designation represented little more than a vague line drawn along the borders between England and Wales. While parish footpaths and public rights of way had meandered alongside the old ditch for twelve centuries, and while Frank Noble insisted this was one of the friendliest of frontiers, parts of the path would be disputed by some land owners who foresaw no benefit in having hordes of Dykers descend on their holdings. Noble, however, did. He believed the path would be an asset to an area that, for all its wild beauty, was as hard pressed as any inner city. He predicted the economic benefits that the Offa's Dyke Path would bring to hard-up, rural businesses, including farming. One hill farming housewife near the Path recalled how, during sheep shearing, she would prepare a midday meal for a dozen and a half shearers, 'meat and vegetables, all done on the open fire see'. In the mid 1960s there was still no mains electricity. By persuading wives like these to offer bed and breakfast Noble convinced many a reluctant farmer to join Offa's cause.

But in the 1960s Noble's main worry was that the rescue attempt of the Dyke Path had come too late. By 1969 new stiles were being erected at the snail's pace of one a year: over 600 were needed. The path was slipping into the undergrowth: rabbits that had nibbled back the vegetation since their introduction by the Romans, had been almost wiped out by farmers who introduced their own rabbits – infected with myxomatosis. And government agencies including the bureaucratic Ministry of Housing and Local

Government, responsible for negotiating the new rights of way were grindingly slow. Noble reported on the funereal pace of progress in 1966. 'In its present condition this National Path is a farce. Some parts of the route resemble an assault course more than a footpath.'

Frank Noble launched an attack. He negotiated the route with landowners. He led teams of volunteers with the Workers Education Association (which he had joined as a tutor) on path clearing days and organised study weekends putting students up in local youth hostels. He set up the Offa's Dye Association in an old school at Knighton to co-ordinate the rescue effort. The Association's ageing duplicator struggled to keep pace with his efforts. Then, one day in 1968, when Noble was working with his volunteers to clear an overgrown section of the Path, he met a group of walkers.

'Where are you going?' he asked.

'Walking Offa's Dyke,' they replied. 'You ought to try it.'

It was the first sign that others were gathering to stretch their legs along Clawdd Offa. Writing his own guide to the Path in 1969, two years before the Path was opened (*The Shell Book of Offa's Dyke Path*) Noble was warning walkers that 'a degree of exploration and pioneering was still necessary to complete the route'. Lord Hunt declared the Dyke Path officially open in 1971. It was, he said, 'not the longest, not the highest, but the best.'

Now dividing his time between the WEA, the

Offa's penny . . . and the symbol of the Offa's Dyke Path Association. (Offa's Dyke Association)

Open University and his beloved Dyke, Noble began to question John Asser's assertion, confirmed by Sir Cyril Fox, that the great rampart really had run from sea to sea. But, as he walked and worked on his thesis, Noble was suffering from the early symptoms of multiple sclerosis. He completed his research confined to a wheelchair, enduring the frustrations of being unable to stride out along his beloved Dyke. Noble died in 1980. He was fifty-four.

The historian, A.J.P. Taylor, himself a keen rambler, had walked most of the Pennine Way, the Ridgeway and, as he put it, most other Ways. But, he wrote in The Listener, 'I say without hesitation that Offa's Dyke is the finest of the lot, even if some of it was the invention of Sir Cyril Fox rather than King Offa. By opening the Dyke, Noble did more for the happiness of mankind than more famous figures.' It was a tribute to the Yorkshire man who loved to walk.

Footnote: The Stile

It's the walker's curse, the farmer's friend and, apparently, a place of assignation for lovers. The stile, from the Anglo Saxon *stigel*, a step or a ladder, is designed to help the walker over a hedge or fence.

So long part of the British countryside, the stile has given rise to some half forgotten proverbs: the best dog leaps the stile first. And Essex stiles, Kentish miles, Norfolk wiles, many a man beguiles (the author presumably came from Suffolk).

From the V-shaped squeezer stile, which permits a

The walker's curse, the farmer's friend and the scene of much 'frolic and merry confusion'. (YHA)

person to pass, but keeps the barrel-bellied sheep at bay, to the traditional kissing gate, the stile, like the hedge, is a British phenomenon. 'This little arrangement is common of these islands is it not?' asks a character in the French novel *Pierre de Coulevain*. Her companion can confirm it so and, warming to her theme, reveals the stile to be a secret meeting place for lovers. In fact, she says, if all the kisses witnessed by the average stile were turned into fairy lamps the stile would be alight with little flames.

William Hone, a radical pamphleteer writing in his *Everyday Book and Table Book* in 1826 bemoaned the disappearing stile. 'Without a jest, stiles and footpaths are vanishing everywhere.' One particular type of stile that was under threat was the country turnstile: 'It is a long time since I saw a turnstile, and I suspect the Falstaff have cried them down,' he declared, explaining the difficulties that stout people encountered when trying to pass through one. He recalled seeing 'a goodly person of some eighteen or twenty stone' becoming held fast in a turnstile that had to be dismantled to set him free.

Hone had a particular reason for regretting the loss of 'even the most inaccessible piece of rustic erection ever set up in defiance of age, laziness and obesity.'The author, it seems was a stile voyeur. 'How many scenes of frolic and merry confusion have I seen at a clumsy stile!' he mused. 'What exclamations and charming blushes, and fine eventual vaultings on the part of ladies, and what an opportunity does it afford to the boys of exhibiting a variety of gallant and delicate attentions.' In short, concluded William Hone, the rude stile was no impediment to rural romance.

TRAILBLAZERS

In the years after the Second World War years everyone seemed to be doing it. And if they were not doing it, they were keen to read the accounts of those who had done it. Walking that is.

In 1969 the Cotswold poet Laurie Lee published his account of a walk to and through Spain on the eve of the Civil War – *As I walked out one Midsummer Morning*. It was 1934 and the nineteen-year-old Lee was escaping the close-knit Cotswold community ('the small tight valley closing in around one, stifling the breath with its mossy mouth') he had eloquently described in *Cider With Rosie*. Lee walked to London carrying a small, rolled-up tent, a change of clothes, a tin of treacle biscuits and the violin, wrapped in a blanket, on which he would depend for his livelihood for the next two years.

Landing at Vigo he walked through central Spain,

through Zamora Valladolid and into Madrid before setting off south through Toledo, Valdepeñas, Cordova and Seville. From here he skirted the coast, now a hot strip of tourist pads and *playa de golf* destinations, then a necklace of impoverished towns and villages. He was bitten by a slavering dog, suffered severe heatstroke, befriended by beggars, bedded by a tender-eyed maiden and, in a final surreal scene, rescued from the impending conflict between the Republicans and General Franco's Fascists by a British destroyer. (He would return to fight with the doomed Republicans who, twice, planned his execution by firing squad because they thought him a spy.)

Other great, and sometimes strange, walking journeys were taken, and written about in the last half of the twentieth century. Eric Newby's *A Short Walk in the Hindu Kush* was neither short nor, from Newby's point of view, especially well planned. Newby, fresh from a career in the London fashion industry bought an expensive pair of Italian boots and set off with a friend from London's Mayfair to the remote Hindu Kush, north east of Kabul. Even before they reached the mountains proper Newby's feet looked as if they had been flayed. Another writer, Dervla Murphy, strode across the globe (or rode to distant counties astride her faithful bicycle, Roz), from India to Madagascar celebrating each journey with another tome. In the 1990s Nicholas Crane who, with his brother Richard had scaled Kilimanjaro on the emerging new breed of mountain bike, devised a walker's route across Britain, reminiscent of one of

Stephen Graham's compass walks. In *Two Degrees West* Crane followed the geographical median line, down through England for 600 km never deviating more than a few metres either side of the meridian.

Again in the 1990s the poet Peter Mortimer walked across Britain with a neighbour's dog and without a penny to his name. In *One Man's Penniless Odyssey* Mortimer wandered from Plymouth to Edinburgh (the dog gave up *en route*) relying on the charity of others: unlike John Taylor and his *Penniless Pilgrimage*, Mortimer had no friendly hosts along the way. (Another penniless traveller, Satish Kumar, made his own pilgrimage for peace in the 1960s when he walked without money through India and Pakistan.)

One of the most renowned walkers, at least at his death in 1996, John Hillaby described himself as a journalist on 'three good local newspapers: the *New York Times*, *Manchester Guardian* and *Hampstead & Highgate Express*', and a regular contributor to *The New Scientist*. His obituary in *The Independent* reported: 'Pedestrian was the last word to apply to John Hillaby, though he has been called the most celebrated pedestrian in England'.

Born in 1917 and brought up in Leeds, Hillaby, in the 1960s, walked from Northern Kenya to Lake Rudolf, armed with good advice from Wilfred Thesiger, and accompanied by hired bearers and a string of camels with character. The resulting book, *Journey to the Jade Sea* set the tone for his

John Hillaby on the Nile.
(Joe Hillaby)

series of walking books, *Journey Through Britain* (a walk from Lands Ends to John O'Groats along green lanes and footpaths), *Journey Through Europe*, and *Journey Through Love* (following the death of his second wife, Tilly, from cancer).

Hillaby prepared for his marathon walks with long hours of research at the London Library 'mining dictionaries and encyclopedias' as he put it, and, after learning that Roman soldiers trained to fight with weapons slightly heavier than those used in battle, walked the London streets carrying a rucksack loaded with a 50 lb (22.5 kg) load of cast iron discs sandwiched between volumes of telephone directories. On his long distance walks he expected his pack to weight in at between 13.5 kg and 18 kg.

In *Journey Home* Hillaby offered an explanation for his densely detailed accounts of his walks. He and his third wife, Katie Burton, were walking to London from Ravenglass in Cumbria by way of his favourite Yorkshire Moors (he kept homes in London and Rosedale on the North Yorkshire moors) when he tripped over his rucksack and broke their breakfast eggs trying to identify a butterfly. (He had been schooled in natural history as a child walking the Pontefract countryside with his grandfather who taught him the names of local plants. A correct identification was rewarded with a chocolate, an incorrect one with a clout across the head.)

The practical and supportive Katie suggested he omit the egg-breaking incident from the book since he could not provide the reader with a positive identification of the butterfly. (Was it a Mountain Ringlet or a Large Heather?) Hillaby, however, gave the account in full because, he explained, he had always been sustained by the belief that everything that happened to him was of general interest. And it was.

His method of dew showering, for example, detailed in *Walking Through Britain*, involved rising from the tent at dawn, and showering in the ice-cold dew that covered the tent's fly sheet. Hillaby was also a cautious advocate of naked walking, striding over Shropshire's Long Mynd during his walk from Lands End to John O'Groats or walking the South Downs on a warm wet day, naked to keep his clothes dry. (On that occasion he encountered a maiden on horseback and had to retreat behind a bush worrying about how he might explain his actions in court.)

Walking, he wrote, is intimate. He held to the view of A.H. Sidgwick (*Walking Essays*) that, while talking requires a definite activity of mind, walking demands passivity. 'Talking tends to make men aware of their differences; walking rests on their identity', declared Sidwick.

Sidwick and Hillaby would have approved of the artist Richard Long who walked for art's sake. Born in 1945 the Bristol artist documented the walks he had taken through the landscape since 1968. He wrote in *A Walk Across England*:

I went down to the sea to start
A walk across England as art.

It was: A WALK OF 382 MILES IN 11 DAYS FROM THE WEST COAST TO THE EAST COAST OF ENGLAND. 'I am content with the vocabulary of universal and common means: walking, placing, stones, sticks, water, circles, lines, days, nights, roads', he explained in *Words after the Fact*.

RECORD BREAKERS

An American, Arthur Blessitt, started walking in September 1969 carrying with him a twelve foot cross. By November 2005 he was said to have walked 37,000 miles (59,544 km) – fifty of the 305 different countries that he crossed were at war at the time – to complete what was then the world's longest journey. (When in 1990 he married an English woman, the couple carried on walking).

Among other record breakers was an American, George Schilling who in 1904 claimed to have been the first person to walk around the world. In 1970 David Kunst made a verified walk around the world. It took him four years and three months to cover 14,450 miles (23,645 km). He set out with his brother John from Waseca, Minnesota on June 20. John was killed in Afghanistan in 1972 when the pair were attacked by bandits. Twenty years later a Suffolk man, John Westley, of Kessingland walked the 9,469 miles (15,239 km) of the British coastline in just over twelve months.

When Ffyona Campbell started her world walk it was 1983 and she was a mere sixteen years old. Over the next eleven years she covered 32,000 km and, although she later rewalked the US section after admitting accepting lifts (she was pregnant at the time), she became the first woman to complete the journey.

But for some, distance was not all. The intrepid Scots poet and author Syd Scroogie, born in 1919, described himself as a hill 'gangrel' or tramp after not only walking the Scottish hills, but making more than 600 ascents of the mountains. This was despite being blinded and losing a leg during the Second World War after stepping on an anti personnel mine in Italy. On that other Celtic frontier in Wales' Snowdonia, Robin Kevan, a retired sixty-year-old social worker from Llanwrtyd Wells walked the hills on a different mission. With a knapsack full of plastic sacks and carrying a litter grabber, Rob the Rubbish as he became known walked to clear litter from places such as Scafell Pike in the Lake District, Ingleborough in the Pennines, Ben Nevis in Scotland and on Snowdon itself. In 2006 he planned a rubbish-collecting trip at Everest base camp.

In 2005 Stephen Gough's choice of a long distance walk, the 874 mile trek from Lands End to John O'Groats took considerably longer than the anticipated two months. This was because the ex-marine from Hampshire insisted on walking with rucksack, boots and socks. And nothing else. As a consequence the naked rambler, who spread more merriment around than most walkers, spent five of the seven-month long journey in prison.

Perhaps the most determined walked of the lot was Karl Bushby. While it was said of Thomas Coryate that 'he went most on foot' it was acceptable practice in 1608 to use the ferry to cross the channel. Not so for Karl Bushby. The former soldier from Hull planned to walk from the southern tip of South America to England, a distance of 36,000 miles (57,960 km) without using any other form of

Karl Bushby starts out
on his marathon walk
around the world.
(Karl Bushby)

transport but his two feet. Working his way towards three major obstacles, the Darien Gap, the semi-frozen Arctic waters of the Bering Straight and the small, but frustratingly deep English Channel. The journey, which promised to take Bushby through some of the world's most challenging terrain in the world for a solo walker, was going to take a while.

Karl Bushby stepped out on 1 November in 1998 from the Chilean town of Punta Arenas. He hoped to be home in Hull in time for Christmas, 2110.

FURTHER READING

n/d – no date
n/p – no publisher

Chapter 1 First footers

A Short Sketch of the Life of Mr Foster Powell (London, R.H.Westley, 1793)

Borrow, George, *Wild Wales* (London, T. Nelson & Sons, n/d)

Crawford, Mabel Sharman, *Through Algeria* (London, n/p, 1863)

Coryate, Thomas, *Coryats Crudities* 1611 (London, Gibson Square Books, 2007)

In Our Age, Vol. 3, Spring 2007 (Herefordshire Lore, Herefordshire County Records Office)

Lithgow, William, *The Totall Discourse of the Rare Adventures and Painefull Peregrinations of Long Ninteen Years Travayles* (1632, n/p)

Michell, John, *The View Over Atlantis*, (London, Garnstone Press, 1969)

Moore-Colyer, Richard, *Roads and Trackways of Wales* (Ashbourne, Landmark Publishing, 2001)

Morris, Mary with O'Connor Larry, editors, *The Virago Book of Women Travellers* (London, Virago Press, 1994)

Muir, Dr Richard, *Shell Guide to Reading the Landscape* (London, Michael Joseph, 1981)

Nicholl, Charles, Field of Bones, *London Review of Books* (2 September, 1999)

Shoesmith, Ron, *Alfred Watkins* (Herefordshire, Logaston Press, 1990)

Terry, Edward, A *Voyage to East India* (London, 1655)

Thom, Walter, *Pedestrianism or, an account of the Performances of celebrated Pedestrians during the past and Present Century; and an Essay on Training* (London, 1813)

Watkins, Alfred, *The Old Straight Track* (London, Methuen & Co. Ltd, 1925)

Williamson, Tom *Dowsing – New Light on an Ancient Art* (London, Hale, 1993)

Chapter 2 Devoted walkers

Attwater, Donald, *The Penguin Dictionary of Saints* (London, Penguin, 1965)

Bingley, Rev'd W., *A Tour Round North Wales performed during the summer of 1798* (1798, n/p)

Bond, Arthur, *The Walsingham Story* (Walsingham, G.J. Selway Guild Shop, 2004)

Bunyan, John, *The Pilgrim's Progress* (London, Collins, 1953)

du Boulay, Shirley, *A Modern Pilgrimage* (London, Moorehouse Group, 1995)

Feltham, John, *A Tour through the Island of Man, 1797, 1798. Letters to Duke of Athol* (n/p, n/d)

Kilvert, Francis, *Kilvert's Diary 1870 – 1879* (London, Century Publishing, 1986)

Marples, Morris, *Shanks's Pony* (London, J.M.Dent, 1959)

Moritz, Carl Philip, *Travels, chiefly on foot, through several parts of England in 1782, 1795* (London, Eland, 1986)

Raleigh, Sir Walter, His Pilgrimage, *Oxford Book of English Verse* (Oxford, Clarendon Press, 1907)

Warner, Rev'd Richard, *Walks through Wales* (1798) and *A Second Walk through Wales* (1799)n/p

Cooper, Canon, *The Tramps of the Walking Parson* (London, Walter Smith Publishing, 1905)

Cooper, Canon, *With Knapsack and Note Book by the Walking Parson*, (London, Brown & Sons, 1910)

Chapter 3 Poets in motion

de Botton, Alain, *The Art of Travel* (London, Penguin, 2002)

Grayling, A.C., *The Quarrel of the Age; the Life and Times of William Hazlitt* (London, Weidenfeld and Nicolson, 2000)

Howe, P.P., ed., *The Complete Works of William Hazlitt* (London, Dent, 1932)

Hucks, John, *A Pedestrian Tour through North Wales in a Series of Letters.* (1795, 1779 n/p)

Street, Sean, *The Dymock Poets* (Bridgend, Seren, 1994)

Thomas, Edward, *The Icknield Way*, (London, Constable, 1916)

The Golden Room and other poems, (London, Macmillan, 1928)

Wordsworth, William, *Guide to the Lakes* (London, Frances Lincoln, 2004)

Wordsworth, Dorothy, The Grasmere and Alfoxden
Journals (Oxford, Oxford University Press, 2000)

Chapter 4 Bringing it to book

Bloomer, Amelia, *True History of the So-Called Bloomer
Costume* (Chicago, Religion-Philosophical Journal
December 1889).

Hall, Edward, Miss Weeton, *Journal of a Governess* (
Oxford, Oxford, 1932)

Hudson, W.H. *Afoot in England* (London, J.M.Dent,
1924)

Hutton, William, *The Life of William Hutton* (1815, n/p)

Oliffe, Hugh, *On Borrow's Trail, Wild Wales Then and
Now* (Llandysul, Gomer, 2003)

Past Forward 21, 22, 25 (Wigan Heritage Services,
1999 – 2000)

Stevenson, Robert Louis, *Travels with a donkey*, (London,
Macmillan, 1955)

Turnbull, Ronald, *The Book of the Bivvy* (Milnethorpe,
Cumbria, Cicerone Press, 2001)

Wordsworth, Dorothy, ed. J.C. Shairp, *Recollections of a
Tour Made in Scotland 1863* (Edinburgh, Edmonston
& Douglas, 1874)

Chapter 5 A walk on the wild side

Clark, Len, *Herbert Gatliff An English Eccentric* (Gatliff
Trust, 1995)

Graham, Stephen, *The Gentle Art of Tramping* (London,
Benn's Essex Library, 1927)

Humphries, Stephen, *Hooligans or Rebels. An oral history of working class childhood and youth 1889 – 193*

(Oxford, Blackwell, 1981)

Maitland, F., Life and letters of Leslie Stephen, (London, n/p, 1906)

Rothman, Benny, *The 1932 Kinder Trespass* (Altrincham, Willow Publishing & Ramblers' Association, 1982)

Stephen, Leslie, *Pleasures of Walking, Studies of a biographer* vol 3 (London, n/p 1902)

Stephenson, Tom ed. Ann Holt, *Forbidden Land* (Manchester, Manchester University Press, 1989)

Chapter 6 Route-masters and record breakers

Crane, Nicholas, *Two degrees West: A Walk along England's Meridian* (London, Viking 1999)

Hillaby, John, *Journey Home* (London, Paladin Books, 1985)

Hillaby, John, *Journey Through Europe* (London, Granada, 1974)

Hone, William, *Everyday Book and Table Book* (London, n/p, 1826)

Lee, Laurie, *As I walked out one Midsummer Morning*, (Penguin Books, 1973)

Mabey, Richard, with Clifford, Susan and King, Angela, *Second Nature* (London, Jonathon Cape, 1984)

Mortimer, Peter, *One Man's Penniless Odyssey* (Edinburgh, Mainstream Publishing, 1999)

Murphy, Dervla, *Muddling Through Madagascar* (London, John Murray, 1985)

Newby, Eric, *A Short Walk in the Hindu Kush*, (London, Secker & Warburg, 1958)

Noble, Frank, *The Shell Book of Offa's Dyke Path* (London, Queen Anne Press, 1969)

Tait, Malcolm, *The Walker's Companion* (London, Robson Books 2004)

Taylor, A J P, *The Listener* (February 12 1981)

The Observer, obituaries (London, 16 September 16 2006)

Trevelyan, George Macaulay Clio, a muse and other essays literary and pedestrian (London Longmans Green and Co, 1913)

Wainwright, A, *Fellwanderer, the story behind the Guidebooks,* (Kendal, Westmoreland Gazette, 1966)

Wainwright, A, *Wainwright In Scotland* (Michael Joseph/BBC, London 1988

Long, Richard, *A WALK ACROSS ENGLAND* (London, Thames and Hudson, 1997

Long, Richard, *Words after the Fact, Touchstones* (Bristol, Arnolfini, 1983)

General

Hillaby, John, Walking In Britain (London, Paladin 1990)

Hogg, Garry, *And Far Away* (London, Phoenix House, 1946)

Somerville, Christopher, *Twelve Literary Walks* (London, W.H. Allen 1985)

Nicholson, Adam, *The National Trust Book of Long Walks* (London, National Trust and Weidenfeld and Nicolson, 1981)

INDEX

Italics denote illustration

Abergavenny , 95
Abergele, 93, 94
Aberglaslyn Pass, 164
Afoot in England, 84, 180–6, 271
Alfoxden, 92, 106, 116, 270
Anderson, Ada, 45
Anglesey, 22, 24. 70, 94, 163
anti–semitism, 204

Bangor, 72, 121, 122, 161, 163, 164
barbed wire, 205
Barclay, Captain, 10, 38–45, *39*, 164
Barmouth, 122
Barnet Fair, 22
baskets, 69
Beaumaris Bay, 163
Beddgelert, 71, 99, 161, 164
Bedford, 26, 57
Belloc, Hilaire, 6, 120, 174–180, *177*, 189
Ben Lomond, 118
Berneray, *234*
Bettws y Coed, 79
Bingley, Rev'd William, 67–73, 75, 269

Birmingham, 11, 61, 142, 144, 148
bivvybag, 172–174
Black Peak, 196
Blaenau Ffestiniog, 164
Bleaklow, 196, 197
Blessitt, Arthur, 264
Blewbury, 125, 127
bloomers, 156–158, *157*
Blue Anchor, 116
Blythe, 137
Borrow, George, 10, 22–24, 134, 158–167, *159*, 271
Bowness, 96
Brecon Beacons, 214
Bredwardine, 76, 77
Bridgwater, 91, 115, 116
Bristol, 73, 94
Bristol Channel, 74, 91, 102, 115, 118, 263
British Workers' Sports Association, 200, 204
bum bag, 69
Bunyan, John, 53–8, 269
Burton, 65
Bushby, Karl, 265–266

Cader Idris, 71, 74–5, 80
Caernarvon, 70, 72, 93
Cambridge, 70, 101, 187, 189
Campbell, Ffyona, 264
camping, 172–4, 228
   tents, 124, 167, 226, 229, 259, 262
Canterbury, 33, 55, 59, 176–9
Capel y Ffin, 76

Cardigan, 79, 121, 122
Carlisle, 26
Carlyle, Thomas, 90
Carmarthen, 24, 25
Castle, Barbara, *213*, 214–15
Castleton, 65, 211
Chelsea, 45
Chepstow, 94, 102, 165
Chester, 120, 161
Chester, John, 92, 116
Cheviots, 208, 214
Chilterns, 127
Chippenham, 76
Clogwyn du'r Arddu, 70
Clyro, 75, 75
Coast to Coast, 247, 248
coffee, 29, 123, 221, 223, 224
Coleridge, Samuel, 11, 59, 60, 92–8, *95*, 99,
    104,119,129, 131, 134
  with Wordsworth, 89–92, 104, 109, 110
  with Hazlitt, 112–18
Colvin, Sidney, 168, 170
compass, 11, 133, 217, 236, 259
  Silva, *219*
communists, 199–200
Cooper, Canon, 12, 81–8, 82, 224, 270
coracles, 72
Coryate, Thomas, 11, 13–19, *16*, 20, 25, 26, 33,
    141, 226, 268
Cotswolds, 127
Cottle, Joseph, 92, 95

Cumbria, 120, 164, 220, 227
  Coleridge, 95
  Hillaby, 262
  Stephenson, 210
  Wordsworth, 99, 104, 105, 107
  Wainwright, 241, 247
Cwm Idwal, 71
Cycling, 56, 83–4, 201, 259

Daily Herald, 206, 211
Dalton, Hugh, *213*, 214
Dartmoor, 220
De Quincey, Thomas, 11, 92, 99, 107, 119–125, *121*, 172
Denbighshire, 70, 72, 121
Derby, 61, 64, 65, 142, 143, 203, 207
Devil's Bridge, 165
dew showering, 262
dogs, 71–2, 163, 167, 217, 256, 259, 260
Dolgellau, 81, 121
Donegal, 220
Dove Cottage, 99, 100, 106, 119
Dover, 14, 178
drovers, 20–5, *21*, *23*, 73, 165
Dunster, 116
Dymock. 130–3, 270

Edale, 196, 197
Edinburgh, 26, 27, 98, 136, 138, 260
Edlesborough, 126
Eldon Hole, 65
Elgar, Edward, 237

Essex, 21, 46, 256

fascists, 200, 259
Feltham, John, 66–7, 69, 133, 269
Field, The, 204
Filey, 81, 83, 85
Forbidden Land, 210, 211, 272
Forest of Bowland, 207, 210
Forest of Dean, 102
Frith, Mary, 45
Frost, Robert, 130–2
Fuller, Bishop, 13, 17

game keepers, 186, 194, 197, 199, *199*, 201–3,
    202, 208
George V, 83
Gloucester, 93, 115, 132, 139
Glyder Fach, 71
Glyder Fawr, 71, *215*
Gog Magog, 127
Gowbarrow Park, 109
Graham, Stephen, 11, 12, 81, 217–225, 259, 271
Grampians, 138, 237
Grasmere, 95, 96, 99, 100, 107, 108, 119, 124, 270,
Greeba, 153
grouse moor, 197, *199*, 204, 208

Hay-on-Wye, 75, 76, 78
Hadrian's Wall, 11, 46, 146–7, 208, 214
Harlech, 79, 121
Hatfield, 26

Hathersage, 194, 196
Hawkshead, 96, 99
Haydon, Benjamin Robert, 101
Hayfield, 201–202
Hazlitt, William, 90, 91, 92, 112–18, *115*, 129, 270
Hereford, 24, 46, 49, 53, 107, 249, 251
Hikers, 192, 196, 198, 208, 214, 219, 226
Hiker and Camper Magazine, 211
Hillaby, John, 12, 133, 240, 241, 260–3, 261, 272, 273
Holyhead, 175
Horseshoe Pass, 162
Horsham, 43
Howarth, 201
Hucks, John, 93–5, 134, 270
Hudson, William (W.H.), 11, 83, 180–6, 205, 271
Hull, 43, 266
Hutton, William, 142–148, 143, 243, 271

Icknield Way, 56, 125–130, 132, 270
Independent, The, 260
inn keepers, 30, 66, 116, 140, 167, 178
Innominate Tarn, 248
Isle of Man, 67, 152–5, 166
Ivinghoe, 126, 128

Joad, Cyril, 195, 196, 197
Jones, Robert, 99, 101–2
Jonson, Ben, 11, 17, 25–27, 27, 28, 33, 46, 52, 136–7, 138
Journal of a Governess, 151, 271

Keswick, 95
Kilvert, Francis, 11, 74–81, 77, 100, 111, 131, 269
Kinder Scout, 10, 197–203, 208
Kirk-Santon, 153
kissing gate, 257
Knettishall Heath, 128
Kumar, Satish, 260
Kunst, David, 264

Lake District, 95, 96, 105, 146, 214, 227, 241,
    242, 245, 265
  guides, 240, 242–3, 246, 248, 270
Lancashire, 44, 45, 209, 244
Landladies, 63, 66, 67, 87, 121, 122, 161, 172, 247
Lao Tsu, 11, 70
Lee, Laurie, 258–9, 272
Lepham's Bridge, 231
Letchworth, 126
ley lines, 50–52
Lichfield, 65
Lindsay, Vachel, 219–222
Lithgow, William, 11, 28–32, 268
Liverpool, 67
Llanberris, 71
Llandovery, 94, 165
Llangollen, 93, 114–15, *117*, 121, 161–2, 164
Llanwrst, 121
Llyn Cwellyn, 163
Lochinver, 247
London, 55, 58, 61, 83, 118, 127, 140, 150, 170, 178,
    179

walking in, 225, 261
walking to, 34, 43, 81, 83, 85, 160, 166, 175, 189, 258, 262
walking from, 25, 26, 33, 34, 44, 65, 88, 136, 141
Long Mynd, 262
Long, Richard, 11, 263
Lourdes, 55–6
Lynton, 91, 116
Lyrical Ballads, 92, 105, 119

Machynlleth, 73, 74, 165
Maidstone, 45
Malvern Hills, *192*, 237
Manchester Guardian, 201, 260
Maps, 49, 50, 66, 133, 135, 145, 152, 176, 179, 182, 200, 208, 242, 244, 247
Marches, 220, 252
Marples, Morris, 82, 269
Menai Straits, 72, 94
Mendips, 127
Meredith, George, 191
Milford Trail, 248
Minehead, 91
Miners, 72, 164
Monkhouse, Patrick, 196, 197
Monmouthshire, 73
Montgomery, 93, 121, 251
Moore-Colyer, Richard, 21, 22, 268
Moritz, Carl, 58, 60–7, 69, 133, 270
Mortimer, Peter, 260, 272

Munro, Hugh, 236–9
Murphy, Dervla, 259, 272

National Parks, 105, 215, 216, 227, 247
Neath, 165
Nether Stowey, 91, 113, 114, 115, 116, 117
Nettlebed, 63
Newmarket, 39, 44, 126
Newport, 74, 165
Noble, Frank, 11, 249–255, 272
North Downs Way, 177, 178
Northampton, 23
Nottingham, 65, 144

Odcombe, 13, 14, 15, 18
Offa's Dyke, 11, 216, 249–255, 272
Old Straight Track, The, 49, 51, 269
Orkney, 28
Orrest Head, 245
Osborne, Fanny, 168, 171, 174
Outer Hebrides, 226, 233, 234, *234*
Oxford, 61, 64, 65, 93, 140, 174, 175, 189, 227

packs, 12, 60, 78, 133–5, 138, 173, 226, 236, 261
    budget, 145, 146
    satchel, 81, 85, 176
pantisocracy, 93
Paradise Lost, 66, 133
Path to Rome, The, 175
Patmore, Peter, 118
Peak District, 60, 61, 64, 196, 207

trespassing, 194, *195*, 197, 198, 207
Pembrokeshire Coast Path, 129, 214, 216
Pendle Hill, 208, 210
Penmaen Mawr, 70, 94
Pennant, Thomas, 251, 252
Pennine Way, 11, 208, 213, 216, 255
Penrith, 146
Perry, Steve, 238–9
pigeon post, 29
pilgrims, 53–8, 58–9, 176–180
Pilgrims Progress, 56–8
Pilgrims' Way, 176–180, *178*, 230
pilgrimages, 26, 28, 53–6, 58–9, 176–9, 221,
    260, 269, 270
Plymouth, 260
Pollock, Sir Frederick, 192, 195
Poucher, William, 236, 239–241, *241*
Powell, Foster, 11, 33–5, 43, 268
Protest, *202*, *203*, 205, 211, 212

Quantock Hills, 91, 104, 127

Ramblers Association, 133, 194–5, 204–5, 209,
    215, 216
rambling, 186, 196, 203, 205, 210, 211, 214
Rhenigdale, 235
Richmond, 61, 65, 190
Ridgeway, The, 127, 255
Right to Roam, 206, 211
robbers, 12, 29, 30, 158, 167, 223
Robin Hood's Bay, 247

Rome, 55, 83, 85–8, 129, 175–6
Ross-on-Wye, 93
Rothman, Benny, 10, 196–205, *198*, 208, 212, 217, 271
Royston, 126, 189
Ruskin, John, 83
Ruthin, 93, 162
Rydal Mount, 104, 106, 111, 119

St Albans, 43
Salisbury, 67
Santiago de Compostella, 56, 59
Schilling, George, 264
Schirrman, Richard, *229*, 230
Scottish Mountaineering Club, 237, 238
Scroogie, Syd, 264
Selworthy Beacon, 116
Shetland, 28
Short Walk in the Hindu Kush, A, 259, 272
Shrewsbury, 112, 113, 114, 115, 121
Snaefell, 154
Snowdon, 71, 79, 94, 99, 151, 163, 200, 265
South Downs Way, 216
Southwell, 144
South-West Peninsular Path, 216
speed walking, 33, 34
Stephen, Leslie, 187–195, 272
Stephenson, Tom, 11, 133, 206–216, *209*, 217, 226, 229, 272
Stevenson, Robert Louis, 10, 60, 112, 134–5, 168–174, *169*, 175, 180, 182

Stockport, 196, 202, 187, 271
Stornoway Gazette, 233
Sunday Tramps, 190, 194
Sutton, 61
Swansea, 25, 165

Tarbet, 108
Taunton, 91
Taylor, John, 18, 26–7, 133, 136–141, *139*, 180, 260
Tenbury Wells, 142
tents, see camping
Terry, Edward, 18, 19
Tewkesbury, 115
Thames, 64, 139, 140
Thetford, 125, 126
Thom, Walter, 38, 42
Thomas, Edward, 56, 125–133, *128*, 270
Tintern, 94, 102–3, 104, 251
Trails, 206, 208, 216, 220, 248
tramps, 88, 224, 234
Travels with a Donkey, *168*, 171–4, 175, 271
Tregaron, 93, 94, 165
trespass, 186, 191–5, 207, 216, 247
  mass trespass, 198, 201–5, 203, 202, 271
  Trespasser's Walk, 217
Trevelyan, George Macaulay, 10, 103, 189, 197,
  204, 230, 273
Tryfan, 71

umbrella, 99, 124, 134, 145, 233
  Borrow, George, 12, 158, 164, 165, *166*, 167

Usk, 74

Vale Crucis, 162, *162*
Von Hillern, Bertha, 45

Waddington Fell, 210
Wainwright, Alfred, 10, 237, 241–9, *243, 244,* 273
Walk Across England, A, 263, 273
walkers
  boots, 36, 37, 69, 219, 222, 259
  clothing 58–60
  head gear, 22, 59, 60, 96, 120, 152, 173, 176,
  224, 242, 249
  shirts, 60, 81, 135, 198, 224, 225
  skirt, 90, 155, 156–8
  socks, 81, 85, 135, 222
  suits, 50, 85, 175, 176
  trousers, 60, 125, 156, 224
  lodgings, 109, 146, 155, 179, 182–3, 229
  rucksack, 12, 232, 233, 261, 262
  best, 223–4
  contents, 133–5, 218, 222–3
  Magazine, 230
  shoes, 14, 55, 88, 98, 164, 222
  sleeping outdoors, 123–4, 137, 172–4, 176, 220, 226
  wet socks, 85
walking,
  clubs, 189, 190–5, 227, *244*
  guides, 240, 241, 242, 245
  health benefits, 38, 70, 111, 189, 228
  honeymoons, 218

journals, 75, 76, 77, 81, 93, 106–111, 145, 151, 159–160, 222, 270, 271
naked, 262, 265
nocturnal, 99, 120, 176, 241, 243
record, 25, 33, 34, 35, 39, 175, 236–241, 264–6
sticks, 26, 59, 81, 85, 94, 175–6, 180
Wallingford, 126
Walsingham, 55, 59, 269
Wanborough, 125, 126
Wantage, 126
Ward, G.H.B. 195
Warner, Rev'd Richard, 67–74, 103, 207
Watkins, Alfred, 46–52, 47, *269*
Watlington, 126
Weeton, Ellen, 148–155
Welshpool, 93
White Peak, 196
Whitney, 78, 107, 111
Wild Wales, 159, 160, 166, 268
wildlife, 184
Williams, Rev'd, 67–72
Winchester, 176, 178, 179, 230–1
Windsor, 61, 62, 65, 83
Winnats Pass, 205, 211, *212*
Wood, Abraham, 44
Wordsworth, Dorothy, 89–92, 97, 98, 104, 106–11, *107*, 270, 271
Wordsworth, William 11, 12, 74, 89–92, 95–6, 97–8, 99, *101*, 111, 113, 116–17, 119, 120, 129
'spots of time', 102, 104, 246

Wrexham, 23, 93, 94
Wye, 76, 102, 104, 165, 251

York, 33–5, 43, 46, 54, 175
Yorkshire Moors
youth hostels, 103, 226-235, 254, *231*, *234*
Yr Wyddfa, *see* Snowdon

Zigzag walk, 225